Hellenic Studies 17

COMPARATIVE ANTHROPOLOGY
OF ANCIENT GREECE

Other Titles in the Hellenic Studies Series

Plato's Rhapsody and Homer's Music
The Poetics of the Panathenaic Festival in Classical Athens

Labored in Papyrus Leaves
Perspectives on an Epigram Collection Attributed to Posidippus
(P.Mil.Vogl. VIII 309)

Helots and Their Masters in Laconia and Messenia
Histories, Ideologies, Structures

Archilochos Heros
The Cult of Poets in the Greek Polis

Master of the Game
Competition and Performance in Greek Poetry

Greek Ritual Poetics

Black Doves Speak
Herodotus and the Languages of Barbarians

Pointing at the Past
From Formula to Performance in Homeric Poetics

Homeric Conversation

The Life and Miracles of Thekla

Victim of the Muses
Poet as Scapegoat, Warrior and Hero in Greco-Roman
and Indo-European Myth and History

Amphoterōglossia
A Poetics of the Twelfth Century Medieval Greek Novel

Priene (second edition)

Plato's Symposium
Issues in Interpretation and Reception

http://chs.harvard.edu

COMPARATIVE ANTHROPOLOGY
OF ANCIENT GREECE

Marcel Detienne

Center for Hellenic Studies
Trustees for Harvard University
Washington, DC
Distributed by Harvard University Press
Cambridge, Massachusetts, and London, England
2009

EDITORIAL TEAM:
Senior Advisers: W. Robert Connor, Gloria Ferrari Pinney, Albert Henrichs,
  James O'Donnell, Bernd Seidensticker
Editorial Board: Gregory Nagy (Editor-in-Chief), Christopher Blackwell,
  Casey Dué (Executive Editor), Mary Ebbott (Executive Editor),
  Scott Johnston, Olga Levaniouk, Anne Mahoney, Leonard Muellner
Production Manager for Publications: Jill Curry Robbins
Web Producer: Mark Tomasko

Articles originally published in *Arion* are reprinted here by permission
  of *Arion* and The Trustees of Boston University.

LIBRARY OF CONGRESS CATALOGING-IN-PUBLICATION DATA
Detienne, Marcel.
Comparative anthropology of ancient Greece / by Marcel Detienne.
  p. cm. -- (Hellenic studies series ; v. 17)
ISBN 978-0-674-02125-9
1. Greece--Civilization--To 146 B.C. 2. Ethnology--Comparative method.
  3. Group identity--Greece--History--To 1500. I. Title.

DF78.D459 2009
938--dc22

2009005009

Contents

Preface:
Doing Anthropology *with* the Greeks

Our history begins with the Greeks.

Ernest Lavisse

ACK IN THE MISTS OF TIME, long before the emergence of articulate language, the human race discovered that it possessed the power to imagine itself other than it was. To begin to be outside oneself, to be transported to another world, all that was needed was a powerful smell or an evocative vision caught by a single intoxicated human being. However, to conceive that the spaces "colonized" by the human race exhibit cultural variation, it would seem that more is required; not only mastery of a rich and complex language but also long, sustained, and thoughtful observation in circles capable of detecting significant differences. America, dubbed the New World several hundred years ago, presents us with "the stupefying spectacle of extremely advanced cultures alongside others at an extremely low technological and economic level. Furthermore, those advanced cultures enjoyed but a fleeting existence: each emerged, developed and perished within the space of a few centuries."[1] In the topmost chamber of a pre-Columbian pyramid, there may perhaps have been a human being, a poet or sage, who did have an inkling that civilizations too are mortal and that others produced concurrently may emerge and be reborn from their own particular cultural productions. Today, the wise men of the United Nations all agree that the development of the human race involves "cultural freedom," the right to choose one's culture or cultures in a world that is becoming increasingly unified yet recognizes its fundamental diversity.

In this volume, I wish to tackle the subject of a comparative anthropology of ancient Greece. Perhaps the first thing to do is explain what I mean by anthropology and how I understand "comparative" in relation both

1 Eribon and Lévi-Strauss 1984:84.

ix

to anthropology and to ancient Greece. The fact that the word anthropology stems from the Greek language does not mean to say that antiquity produced a body of "knowledge" or discourse, a *logos*, on human beings in general that was peculiar to "anthropologists" in the same way as, for example, there are *theologoi*, or "theologians," so called because they write about either the gods of their own homelands or those of neighboring cities.[2] In the fourth century BCE, Aristotle remarked that "anthropologist" was the word applied to a chatterbox, someone with an excessive gift of the gab; a somewhat unpromising start![3] It was not until the eighteenth century CE, a little before the time of Immanuel Kant, that, in Europe, we find the first signs of a body of knowledge called anthropology, which, in 1788, was so designated by Kant himself. Subsequently, and more important, there emerged scholarly societies such as that of the "Observers of Mankind" (1799), mankind in all its diversity, in the astonishing variety of the "civil societies" or, as we should now say, its "cultures." I am using culture in the technical sense that this word acquired with Edward B. Tylor. Tylor was one of the great English founders of anthropology-as-a-science, which encompassed beliefs, practices, and technology— everything that we consider to be covered by morality, law and art, customs, and mores—all that the human beings (of both sexes) who make up a society receive and pass on, transforming it as their creativity and choices dictate, insofar as the latter are accepted by that society.[4]

That was how anthropology began. Now, what about "comparative anthropology"? The study of cultural diversity in the history of our species must necessarily involve comparison between so many strange cultural phenomena. Anthropology was born comparative. To be sure, it was neither the first nor the only "discipline" to resort to comparison. Already in the sixteenth century, freethinking minds in Europe were bold enough to compare different religions. They noted resemblances, drew attention to differences, and ventured to raise pertinent questions about the shared common ground and beliefs held to be revealed truths in more than one religion.[5] Beneath the leaden skies of an absolutism at once spiritual and temporal, this was a subversive operation, and one that was extremely risky for those who undertook it. To shed light, be it that of a single candle, on the different ways of reading a book

2 Pépin 1971:1–51. On"*theologia*" or the meaning of *theologos* see Goldschmidt 1970:141–172 and also Bodéüs 1992:115–167, 301.

3 Aristotle, *Nicomachean Ethics* IV, 8, 1125a5.

4 References in Copans 1996; others, many of them very suggestive, are to be found in Izard and Bonte 1991.

5 Eg. de la Boullaye 1922:151–175; Borgeaud 2004.

of revelation, of querying the traditional view, or of venturing on an interpretation was to invent a new comparative history of religions. The admirable blossoming of "heresies," those remarkable choices made in the springtime of the Reformation, encouraged that invention, albeit without challenging the authority of the book known as the Bible or that of its many clergies.

It was also in the sixteenth century that human beings began to investigate their own species. Henri de la Popelinière and Jean Bodin, those ever-young "historians," rose at dawn to embark on a feverish comparison between the mores and customs of the ancients and the "Gallic Republic" with those of the New World. At a time when historians had not yet acquired any professional status, the most visionary of them dreamed of taking to the high seas to discover and experience such different and fascinating "civil societies" (or "cultures," as we should say). Other comparative approaches were also to emerge, among them the "reconstructions" of the first quarter of the eighteenth century, some of which were designed to establish a genealogy of the mind, others to situate recognized civilizations on an evolutionary scale. The first ventures into paleontology, geology, archaeology, and biology all practiced comparative methods that afforded glimpses of the deep-rooted history of the human species and disclosed the immense richness of cultural phenomena on a global scale.[6]

As soon as anthropology gained recognition as a science—Tylor had called it the "Science of Civilization"—it set about posing questions of a more general nature. These concerned kinship rules, forms of social organization, and systems of representation. Anthropology was born between 1860 and 1880; and, it must be stressed, right from the start it took a radically comparative form. It chose to place in perspective so as to study not only ancient societies, the medieval European past and some, at least, of our contemporary mores and customs, but also primitive civilizations across the world. The first person to be given a professorial chair of social anthropology in Europe—indeed, in the world—was the author of *The Golden Bough.* James George Frazer, a Hellenist who had edited and written a scholarly commentary on *The Description of Greece* by Pausanias, a traveler in the reign of Hadrian who set off to discover the cults and traditions of Greeks in times past.[7] But the skies soon darkened as the first "great nations," France, Germany, and Britain, appeared on the scene and as, concurrently, history, pompously labeled "historical science," was institutionalized

---

6 Allow me to refer the reader to Detienne 2000b:17–39 ("Si d'aventure un anthropologue rencontre un historien," which is still relevant).

7 See Ackerman 1987.

and took to preaching from its professorial pulpit. Once ensconced, it appro-
priated as its own domain one subject in particular: "nationhood," which had
first received its political and legal credentials in the 1850s. The task for professional historians on university payrolls was to establish "scientifically" that all
great nations depend inherently on the manner of their genesis.[8] In 1905, the
sociologist Emile Durkheim remarked, with some distaste, that it was impossible to analyze "the obscure, mystic idea" of a "Nation" scientifically.[9] With
pre-1914 foresight (he was, after all, to become the moral conscience of the
French motherland), this same scholar argued that "nationhood" was not at all
a good subject for a sociologist; by reason of its very unique character, it ruled
out comparison. According to Durkheim, comparison had to be constructive.
That is to say, it was essential for work on social types in order to pick out their
common characteristics, to contrast their respective systems and contexts, and
then to observe and analyze their invariant features.[10] Around 1870, historical
science forged a national and exclusive type of history, extolling its incomparability, in both senses of that term: such history was superior to every other kind
and, furthermore, could not be viewed comparatively, as was demonstrated
by the example of France and Germany, facing each other on either side of the
Rhine. The orientation of the discipline of historical science could not fail to
draw attention to the distance that set it apart from anthropology, which, in
contrast, was entirely committed to the exercise of comparison.

Given that my purpose is to set out, in the simplest possible terms, a
plan for a comparative anthropology of ancient Greece, we must now see how
the Greeks fared after Frazer and his Cambridge associates, who proceeded
to merge anthropology with Hellenism.[11] Who were these Greeks? How
important are they? In order to determine the places assigned to the ancient
Greeks in a field marked out in terms of the tension that existed between a
highly nationalistic "historical science" and an anthropology committed to
comparison, it is important to focus on one essential point that affected the
gap that was increasingly to separate the two disciplines. It was in that same
nineteenth-century period that an initially insidious and then definitive split
appeared, separating societies said to be "without writing" from societies
that were endowed with, and soon glorified, writing—writing without which,
it was claimed, there could be no "civilization."[12]

---

8 See Detienne 2003: 123–149 ("Grandeur du français raciné").
9 Durkheim 1975:160–163; 178–224.
10 See Durkheim 1937:124–138.
11 See esp. Detienne 2001.
12 See Detienne 2000a. For reflections on "historical discourse/ethnological discourse," see

The cultures newly discovered between the sixteenth and the nineteenth centuries have been grouped together under a variety of headings; primitive societies, savage societies, and societies not yet civilized. When, in 1868, in France, the institution of the Hautes Etudes was created alongside the university, one extremely controversial department gathered under its secular aegis all the known religions, in order to analyze them as different species of one and the same genus. But in 1888, a chair of "The Religions of Non-civilized Peoples" was created alongside that of "The Major Religions," the foremost of which was, and still is, Christianity, in particular in its hard-core version: Catholicism. It took many years of ardent struggle to gain recognition of the right to "religion" for the group of peoples lacking civilization. It was, I am convinced, when, even before Maurice Leenhardt, this chair was occupied by Marcel Mauss, surrounded by his Africanist, Indianist, and Oceanist disciples, that it became the vibrant focus for anthropological thought. Leenhardt's successor, Claude Lévi-Strauss, has told us how, at the suggestion of his listeners from what the French, curiously, called "overseas," he changed the name of his chair to "The Religions of Peoples Without Writing." "Without writing" then came to be regarded as the self-evident feature in ethnology, which, in Europe, soon came to be regarded as devoted essentially to societies for the most part ruled by oral tradition and supremely indifferent to writing and other graphic signs.[13]

As the eighteenth century and, a fortiori, the nineteenth saw it, it was impossible to spread civilization among peoples of nature if they remained illiterate: for civilization, writing was indispensable. Written texts constituted the essential mark of historical societies, the kind that made history, about which historians had to write, particularly now that they had become the professional practitioners of a real "science." Noncivilized peoples, "without writing," had to be considered likewise "without history," a fact that the Age of Enlightenment had discovered and that the nineteenth century then turned into a dogma. The newly born historical science had no doubts that its proper object was to analyze written documents, archives, and testimonies transmitted by writing. The task of history was to study and understand civilized societies whose ancient status could be deduced from readable written signs. Even today, in the scholarly disciplines of nations now mere provinces of a federated Europe, some societies are designated "for ethnologists," others "for historians." Those historians are ten or fifteen times more

---

Duchet 1985. On "Anthropology and History" (yesterday and today in France), see above all Lenclud 1987.
13 Lévi-Strauss 1968:1–4.

numerous and more powerful than the anthropologists, to whom, nevertheless, France's Ministry of (so-called) National Education generously allots the intellectual management of some 6,000 of the 6,500 cultures known to us.

In between history on the one hand and anthropology on the other, where, I again ask, do the Greeks stand? They belong to the group of ancient peoples but likewise to that of societies that have also been classed as archaic, ever since Lewis Morgan compared "types of family relationships" among Indian, Greek, Germanic, and Polynesian tribes.[14] The very idea of classifying the Greeks of Homer and Plato among the noncivilized peoples soon came to be considered scandalous, not to say unthinkable. Across the board, from Winkelmann to the German romantics, Greek philosophy and literature lay at the very heart of whatever was meant by civilization. So how should we envisage a project such as a comparative anthropology of ancient Greece? We are at this point reaching the very nub of the question of a comparative approach. Once historians of the France "before" France and the Germany "before" Germany appeared, nationalism became the dominant feature in the early form of historical science. Even today, after more than a century of a so-called common education, the history that is taught in the French mother tongue remains fundamentally nationalistic. After World War I, even Durkheim accepted that "our [that is, French] history" had a universal significance. In the 1980s, Fernand Braudel, a quintessential historian, took over from Ernest Lavisse and Maurice Barrès. But it was Lavisse who first realized the important role that a myth of origins played in founding a history of the nation.

In his *Instructions*, Lavisse declared that what secondary-school pupils need to be taught, without their realizing it, is that "our history begins with the Greeks."[15] Our [French] history begins with the Greeks, who invented liberty and democracy and who introduced us to "the Beautiful" and a taste for "the Universal." We are heirs to the only civilization that has offered the world "a perfect and as it were ideal expression of justice and liberty."[16] That is why our history begins, has to begin, with the Greeks. This belief was then compounded by another every bit as powerful: "The Greeks are not like Others."[17] After all, how could they be, given that they were right at the beginning of our history? Those two propositions were essential for the creation of a national mythology that was the sole concern of traditional humanists and historians, all obsessed with nationhood. The major nations of Europe, each in its own way, share the

14 Morgan 1877.
15 Ernest Lavisse, *Instructions de 1890*, cited in Furet 1982:119–120.
16 A notion expressed over and over again, most recently in de Romilly and Vernant 2000:5–28.
17 Detienne 1975:3–24; 1998b.

belief that their own histories also—thank goodness—originate in the values of Greece and that their Greeks are, naturally, beyond compare. Anthropologists of Greece who had the effrontery to compare the mythology and thought of the Greeks with the risqué stories of the savages of America and Polynesia were promptly marginalized, if not well and truly excommunicated.[18] Today, as no doubt tomorrow too, it is commonly accepted among Hellenists and antiquarians both in Europe and in the United States that Greece remains the birthplace of the West and of all the values that conservatives the world over defend with equal vigor. Once scattered in tribes throughout a thousand and one motley cities, the Greeks have become our Greeks: in them our Western autochthony must be founded and rooted.

By thus appropriating the Greeks, the nationalistic historians of the West seem to have definitively removed the ancient societies of Greece from the domain of the scholarship of anthropologists who, in Europe, are few enough anyway and who, in the New World, are woefully inadequately informed of what is at stake.[19] For in truth, much certainly is at stake for comparative studies in our multicultural world and for the kind of anthropological thought that challenges both incomparability and the West's declared claim that it has always been exceptional on account of its purely Greek values.

Paradoxically enough, the impression that the Greeks are our closest neighbors, which some of our "humanists" may nurture, is based on common issues and categories, many of which are precisely those on which early comparative anthropology decided to focus. As I have noted above, the founders of anthropology, while being imbued with the very best kind of Englishness, laid the bases for the "Science of Civilization" by proceeding from descriptions of the Aboriginal Australians to the treatises of Plutarch, and from the mythology of the Iroquois to reflections on the myth of Xenophanes, the philosopher of Colophon. Out of this dialogue that the young anthropologists of the nineteenth century set up between ancient Greeks and primitive peoples emerged major issues for the new discipline and excellent questions on the basis of which we can, as I hope to show, involve ourselves in comparative anthropology *with* the Greeks, possibly adopting a new methodology.

Let me begin by listing a few of those issues, briefly indicating why they are relevant today. The first is myth, along with mythology and "mythical thought." Then come the relations between orality and writing. Next, those

18 Detienne 1978.
19 As is shown, despite his philosophical understanding of "multiculturalism," by Taylor 1992.

between philosophy and wisdom, and the question of truth. And finally, the origin of politics and the invention of "Democracy."

One early line of thought about the nature of myths and their meaning in the history of the human race unfolded in the eighteenth century, with Fontanelle and Lafitau, around the "fable" of the Greeks and the Americans. Today, as in the past, debates on "primitive thought" or "mythical thought" are inseparably linked with the status of mythology as recognized among the ancient Greeks.[20] Whether they appear as mutants or as mediators, the Greeks of antiquity seem to present in their culture, or at least in that of Homer and the eighth century, a state of civilization midway between forms of orality and the already diversified practices of writing. Should those early Greeks be classified among the societies "with" writing or those "without"? For historical science and the tribe of historians as a whole, that is an important question, and much research has been devoted to a comparison between different types of oral poetry and oral practices generally. Meanwhile, anthropologists working with certain doughty Hellenists have successfully explored and compared the effects of the introduction of writing in a wide range of different types of societies in which new subjects for intellectual consideration have emerged.[21] In the land of Pythagoras and Parmenides, philosophy and wisdom were always considered to be indigenous. The invention of philosophy was absolutely and emphatically claimed by archaic Greece, while ancient China was allowed a monopoly over wisdom. Clearly, the Seven Sages were never consulted on the matter, and comparative studies set out to qualify such a simple-minded dichotomy by dint of analyses of a series of microconfigurations encompassing, for instance, "places and names allotted to truth" in both "philosophy" and other forms of knowledge.[22]

Finally, the figure of the statesman and the image of politics, which seem to be exclusively Greek, if not Athenian, are discoveries apparently indispensable to any inquiry into social systems in Africa and India. They are equally so to any attempts to understand the various other forms of power that Aristotle and other excellent observers of the human race identified. In the United States, as in Europe, it is commonly said that it was in Greece that Democracy (with a capital D) fell to earth from the heavens. But among entrenched scholars and the ignorant alike, far less is known of what we might learn from a comparative approach to practices that produce "something akin to politics" in all the

---

20 See Detienne 2003c:3–28, "From Myth to Mythology."
21 See Detienne 1994b.
22 See Detienne 1996:15–33.

hundreds of small societies—communities, cities, chiefdoms, ethnic groups, and tribes—that are scattered throughout the world.[23]

It would not be hard to add further themes to those mentioned above: for example, history (*historia*), in the Greek Herodotean sense of an "inquiry" that produces historicity and its attendant forms of historiography. This constitutes a field of strategic research into a type of anthropology with (that is to say "using") the Greeks that should call into question the assumptions of a historiography trapped by Occidentalism as much as by the nationalistic framework of early historical science."[24] Linked closely to the theme of history is that of autochthony, equally Greek but as yet hardly touched, despite the fact that it leads directly to a number of ways of "carving out a territory," one of which, very familiar to our twenty-first century contemporaries, is known as claiming a "national identity."[25] As is shown by the above list of themes, comparative anthropology focuses on problems. It is wary of intuitive approaches and impressionistic comparisons, and it challenges commonplace generalizations. So it is important to determine precisely what approach to adopt, what method to follow, as we say, after having tried to map out some kind of orientation—no doubt one of many that would be equally illuminating.

The comparative approach that I am championing and hope to illustrate here is fundamentally a joint operation between ethnologists and historians. It is both experimental and constructive.[26] In accordance with the customary demarcation lines between disciplines, anthropologists and historians have become accustomed to living and thinking in separate worlds: worlds separated by prejudices as futile as that inherited from the nineteenth century which set societies "without history" apart from those "with." Nothing but intellectual laziness is preventing a comparative approach from developing between historians and anthropologists working together. After all, is it not up to them, between them, to promote an understanding of all the human societies and cultures in the world, across both time and space?

Regarding method, I should stress how important it is for a comparatist to be at once singular and plural, but what kind of a comparatist do I have in mind? One who takes shape thanks to an intellectual network woven to

---

23 See "Des comparables sur les balcons du politique," in Detienne 2005: 145–176 *passim*.

24 For an initial approach, allow me to refer the reader to Detienne 2000b:61–80 ("Mettre en perspective les régimes d'historicité").

25 This is the subject of my book *Comment être autochthone: Du pur athénien au français raciné* (2003).

26 Following "Construire des comparables" (Detienne 2000b:41–59), I returned to this subject in Detienne 2002a, hoping to attract the attention of a few anthropologists if not of certain historians. See also a paper aimed at Anglo-Saxon readers, Detienne 2002c.

include a number of ethnologist-historians and historian-ethnologists. The enterprise—and that is certainly the word for it—may be undertaken by a couple of scholars working together, one a historian, the other an anthropologist, provided each shares the intellectual curiosity and skills of the other. We should, then, work together, in groups of two or four, but each of us must believe that it is as important to be sustained by the knowledge and questions of our partners as it is to analyze in depth the society for which each of us, either as an anthropologist or as a historian, has chosen to become a "professional" interpreter. There can be no doubt that a regular attendance at seminars disposes people to think together and out loud. Working together in a mixed group comprising both ethnologists and historians: well, you might ask, what is so new about that?

It has been ages since ethnologists and historians met up and began to move forward in convoy. Traveling in convoy certainly implies keeping an eye on one another as you navigate. You observe your companions, rub shoulders with them, sometimes borrowing a subject (immediately dubbed "a new subject") or an expression that provokes an agreeably exciting feeling that you are thinking in a new way. The way that anthropology stands back from its object and views it from afar is both unsettling and attractive to history, particularly if, perchance, glancing in the mirror one morning, the latter decides that it looks somewhat jaded, less beautiful, a touch more ponderous than it used to. The two disciplines usually enjoy a flirtation, but seldom a full-blown relationship. Their more serious practitioners soon return to their own affairs. Historians make the most of the opportunity to reassert that they prefer to compare among themselves, with their close and longstanding neighbors. The wiser among them even acknowledge a certain weakness for fine similarities and analogies. But there is no getting around the fact that the fervent advice of the entire establishment—clergy, academies, and all the institutions that really count—is that history should not take ethnology as its bedfellow. Ethnology is, of course, alluring, but really not from the same social bracket. Besides, rumor has it that it does not have much of a future: out of work today; and tomorrow, without the necessary official credentials, who knows? We have been warned by our elders: this is not the way to end up with a seat in the academy.

Nevertheless, I persevere: can comparative studies amount to a profession? And the answer is yes; one can be a professional comparatist, even an experimental and constructive one. Experimental? In what sense? As historians and ethnologists working together, we can pool a wealth of knowledge about hundreds, even thousands of different cultures and societies ranging across both space and time.[27] I am fully convinced that our common task is to analyze human societies and to understand as many of their cultural products as possible. Why not "experiment" on the basis of "earlier experiments," given that this is both possible and acts as an excellent stimulus to the intellectual activity of historians and anthropologists alike? It involves working freely together for years, moving from one society to another, always in the indispensable company of experts, specialists in each particular terrain. Without the active commitment of a collaborating group, a little laboratory of ethnologists and historians on the move, a group constantly renewed, there can be no comparative approach that is at once experimental and constructive.

There seems to me to be little point in arguing about whether it is more profitable to compare "what is close" or "what is distant."[28] The one does not exclude the other. All the same, I do believe that comparative studies is more vibrant and more stimulating if ethnologists and historians are able and willing to lend an ear to dissonances that at first seem "incomparable," and to put them in perspective. By dissonance I mean, for example, a case where a society appears to make no room for an institution or configuration that our kind of common sense regards as normal and natural, or where a system of thought encountered elsewhere does not appear to offer any obvious category.

Once a historian or an ethnologist, trained to work on some local and precise problem, reaches the conclusion that our notion of what "personality" is constitutes a rather unusual idea within the framework of all the cultures in the world, he or she really is beginning to think as an anthropologist,[29] or is at least taking the first steps in that direction. The next step might entail the discovery that "the better to analyze the symbolic forms of a foreign culture, you have to delve into the cast of mind of another people."[30]

Here we come to the nub of the matter. To experiment and then to construct what it is that ethnologists and historians are together going to compare, you have to pick out a concept or category. It should be neither too

---

27 The comparative approach that I am championing is thus different from that practiced by Georges Dumézil and Claude Lévi-Strauss, both of whom declare that nothing should be compared unless it can be related to a common history, that is to say, for the former, the domain of Indo-European languages, for the latter, the historical and geographical unity of America.

28 Valensi 2002.

29 I am inspired here by an example in Geertz 1983:64–70. Particularly given that in Europe, in the 1960s and 1970s, "personality" was a subject greatly favored by those practicing a comparative approach, a fact of which American anthropologists continue to be unaware. See, for example, Meyerson 1973.

30 Geertz 1983:64–70.

parochial and specific nor too general and comprehensive. An example, to which I will be returning at length, may show what I mean by "to experiment" and "to be constructive." In an inquiry undertaken twenty or so years ago, I, along with a small group of Hellenists and Africanists, wondered how we could produce a comparative analysis of an action as common and as interesting as that of "founding."[31] The first phase of experimentation involves discovering societies or cultural groups that provide models of types and practices of "foundation." How does one set about "founding" in Vedic India or in the societies of West Africa? In all likelihood, in different and contrasting ways. All the members of the little group of researchers thereupon feel free to branch out from the societies closest to their own chosen terrains and to go off in search of cultures and societies that are in principle "untouchable" for any self-respecting historian or strictly correct ethnologist trained never to wander from his or her particular cultural area or particular adopted community.

That is the first move to make. The second comes hard on its heels, once the group members begin to venture further afield and travel from one culture to another, frequently between ones that are separated by vast distances. This is the surest way to discover a society in which there seems to be no equivalent of "founding" or "foundation." The local experts are categorical: in the society of which they are the historians or ethnologists, "there is no such thing as founding": there is simply restoration, ceaseless restoration. What is discovered seems to be a perfect dissonance: a category that seemed commonsensical more or less everywhere begins to waver and soon crumbles away.

The comparatists, now on the alert, immediately begin to wonder: what is it that we ascribe to "founding" that makes it a very particular way of doing something that amounts to not just "inhabiting" or "being in a certain space," but "establishing a territory"? "Establishing a territory" may involve certain forms of autochthony of a native or aboriginal character and also ways of inhabiting a particular place after arriving from outside or elsewhere.

"Founding" was not a bad point of entry. "Establishing a territory" was an even better one—above all a better way to begin to construct what can be compared. What, after all, is the meaning that we ascribe to "founding," to "being autochthonous" or "aboriginal"? If we set about analyzing a series of very different ways of "establishing a territory," we begin to pose questions that soon branch out in two main directions: On the one hand, what is the meaning of to begin, to inaugurate, to historicize, to historialize? On the

---

31 This is the clearest example, and I used it in *Comparer l'incomparable* (2000b:44–56), on the basis of my remarks in Detienne 1990.

other, what does it mean to be born in a particular place, to be a native, to be called indigenous, to have or not to have roots? And what is a place? What is a site? The comparatists, alerted by one or more dissonances, then proceed to coin a new category or set of concepts. They move constantly from one culture or society to another if these seem of a kind to make the conceptual elements that have been discovered productive. They try to see how known cultural systems react not only to the initial category that was selected as a touchstone but also to the series of questions that now arise and the conceptual elements that gradually come to light.

So "our history" does not begin with the Greeks. It is infinitely vaster than a single territory such as France and the beliefs of its accredited authorities. Rather, let us do anthropology with the Greeks: that is the invitation to a voyage offered by this book, which aims to discover at least some aspects of the art of constructing some kind of comparability.

PART I

Murderous Identity

1

The Art of Founding Autochthony:
Thebes, Athens, and Old-Stock French*

Yes, THERE IS AN ART in founding what some call their roots and others autochthony. I have chosen this approach, valid both for the present and the past, for two reasons. These have to do with two complementary lines of inquiry, two systems of collective thought which concern both historians and anthropologists, including those who are at present studying contemporary phenomena in societies far distant from one another.

The first line of inquiry, which began about fifteen years ago, was directed at the ways of creating a territory, and aimed at answering the question, apparently so simple: *what is it to found?* Rather than trying to make a typology of founding or to draw up a morphology of founding, it has seemed to me more interesting first to ask the question,what do we invest in the art of founding which seems to be at the heart of establishing territory? Very likely this would involve the uniqueness of a specific space identified by a name, with individual features and boundaries assigned within a larger space. To which must be added a beginning in time, in history, in chronology, with something like an initial event that is separate, recognized, extraordinary, even solemn. Founding seems to require a significant start, ready to become part of the flow of historic process. Finally, in thinking of founding, we are alluding to an act, a group of gestures, a ritual or a ceremony inseparable from an individual who is at the origin of the ties with, the rootedness in, this place that is considered unique. This first collective line of inquiry inspired me to look into the roads taken by Apollo and to follow this founding god who wanders, knife in hand, among the first Greek cities established after the sanctuary at Delphi.[1] To think comparatively is, quite simply, to engage in a conceptual analysis of what it means "to establish territory in terms of founding by doing the

* This chapter is a revision of an article published in *Arion* 9.1 (Spring/Summer 2001) 46–55.
1 Cf. Detienne 1998a.

rounds," with these questions in mind and in the company of a number of friendly informants from societies which are more or less in the process of establishing their territory.[2] Some of these will be doing so by means of hard-core founding, others by purely and simply setting up a viable economy. The most disparate societies are also those that inquirers find the most stimulating—given their "incomparability."

The second and most recent line of inquiry has its point of departure in a question similar to the first: *how does one become autochthonous?* That is a question that should bewilder the brains of all old-stock Athenians, Serbs, or French. Indeed, *how can one be rooted?* a nomad wondered on the evening after a long day's march. This is a good opportunity to suggest that autochthony, as it was understood by Herodotus, Plato, or Euripides, and yes, the autochthony of yesterday and today, is being continuously established and reestablished. Historians and mythologists never stop laboring to increase its importance. Especially in those cases where autochthony declares itself to be pure and claims to be born of itself and itself alone, it admits that it needs what gives it foundation, roots, quite as much as it needs what goes into building it up. How does one become autochthonous? How can one call oneself old stock? By taking a special look at the comings and goings between Athens and Thebes, it is possible to reflect on the strong ties made by nationalist tribes between the cult of roots and a religion of the dead, between heritage and heredity. To a French ear, The Earth and the Dead reverberates far back into the past, while the German version *Blut und Boden* still freezes the blood of those born a little before the author of *Mein Kampf* executed his mad plans for conquest and destruction.[3] Like many others I was delighted when Germany renounced that right of birth which made *homo germanicus* so detested. Is the phrase The Earth and the Dead so redolent of Maurice Barrès that it is no longer in current use? For at least the last two hundred years Europe, old and new, has once again been inhabited by the dreams of nations whose history, it appears, is unique, cannot be compared. There is France, with its powerful extreme Right always ready to join forces around its old-stock Frenchman.[4] In the former Yugoslavia, we saw pictures on our television screens every evening of Serbs intoxicated by the idea of a Greater Serbia, declaring loud and clear as they set out (it was in the summer of 1999) that they would return to Kosovo, to the land consecrated by the blood of their ancestors—the blood spilled six centuries earlier in a battle lost to the

2 One of the last: Liberski-Bagnoud 2002.
3 Barrès 1899; Glaser 1978:151–161; Linke 1999.
4 Cf. Robichez 1997, with several quotations from Braudel 1986. More in Detienne 2003a:121–149.

Turks. Next door is Hungary with its post-Soviet rituals of reburial,[5] Romania with its cult of the earth hallowed with its children, not to mention Holy Russia, or the modern state of Israel discovering the symbolic power of tombs which establish the rootedness of its people, those tombs of the patriarchs found on the West Bank and which, very opportunely or very unfortunately according to your point of view, give a rootedness to Palestinian autochthony.

I have evoked the old-stock Frenchman who, almost ten years ago, invaded the demography of France, because he seems to me to lead us straight to the Athenian, who is just as much old stock. In its first manifesto, the National Front, this jewel in the crown of the extreme Right on French soil, recalled the incomparable character of the French people: this community bonded by race and memories in which a man can flourish. He belongs to it because of his roots, his dead, the past, heredity, heritage. There you have the old-stock Frenchman whose greatness blazes forth today among the *allogènes*, the old-stock Frenchman who can trace his lineage back to the hunter-gatherers of the Dordogne without interruption.[6]

Direct by way of our Greeks. Mythology has seen stranger things. One word of explanation, though, for the *allogènes*. In his *Cahiers* Maurice Barrès, the inventor of that very French watchword The Earth and the Dead, noted that one needed two elements in order to make a nation: cemeteries and history lessons. In other words: some dead men to provide roots, some historians to get the dead to speak, and then some illustrious dead to weave a continuity. That is the first principle of the history of France such as it has been written from Michelet on, the tradition being handed down from one chaired historian to the next. The most famous of these, and certainly the one whose view of the rooted Frenchman has been the most lasting, is Ernest Lavisse, now a national monument.[7] An exemplary historian indeed, and in his instructions for the teaching of the history of France, he said—and so it was done—that we should learn that our history begins with the Greeks.[8] Which Greeks? Not those of the Black Sea or the Thracian colonies, but the Athenians, the pure-blood Greeks, the Greece *of sang épuré* in that noble seventeenth-century phrase.

Let us go back in time and take our leave of Ernest Lavisse, patron saint of that official history which led us to the heart of the mythology of autochthony. Let us see how it unfolded in its golden age, in the Athens of the first half of the fourth century BCE, when the political orators of that time,

5 Losonczy and Zempleni 1991.
6 Cf. Robichez 1997.
7 Cf. Nora 1997.
8 Quotation from Furet 1982:119–120.

holding a position comparable to that of history professors of the nineteenth and twentieth centuries, were invited to make every breast swell with pride and love of nation. How do these Bossuets of the Athenian funeral oration successively define their precious Athenian identity down throughout a century?[9]

A sketch may be drawn with three strokes: (1) We are the autochthons, born of that very earth we have inhabited since the beginning of time. We are the genuine autochthons, born of an earth whose inhabitants have been the same from their origins, without any break. It is a land which our ancestors have passed on to us; heritage, heredity, the past, in a direct line. (2) The Others: all other cities are made up of immigrants, foreigners, people from elsewhere, and their descendants are the *metoikoi* 'the aliens,' in the Athenian sense of the word, which is not quite the same as ours but which is just as derogatory. So, outside Athens, it is clear: there are composite cities, towns with a mishmash of every origin. Only the Athenians are pure autochthons, pure in the sense that their blood has not been mixed with or contaminated by foreign blood.[10] These are phrases that resound in the *Menexenus*, which, although a pastiche of funeral orations, is a truer one than all the speeches made before or after Plato. Our city feels pure unadulterated hate for the tribe of foreigners, declares the ringing voice of Aspasia-Socrates, invited to make the funeral oration that year.[11] (3) The place of the dead given back to the earth: our ancestors, inhabiting from time immemorial their mother-fatherland, were nourished by the Earth. So they have made it possible for their sons, once they have died, to repose in the familiar places of Her who brought them into the world and gave them suck. For, let us note in passing, the female body is given a place of honor, what with Mother Earth, Earth as Matrix, the mother who bore Ericthonius, the first Athenian autochthon, and opposite her, Athena, the woman of power, the trenchant goddess, hard as a lance.

In mythology, as elsewhere, every detail is important. For example, what if we want to understand how a specific configuration of autochthony has been constructed when its foundation element has been discreetly erased by the moderns, as in certain versions by the ancients? Let us return to the *Bibliotheca* said to be by Apollodorus.[12] It begins by recalling that the gods, one fine day, discover that men have invented the city, and even a number of cities. So the cities are there; the gods neither plan towns nor found cities for mortals. At a later date, the gods decide to take possession of the political establishments

---

9 Cf. Loraux 1981.
10 Cf. Detienne 2003a:19–59 ("Une authochtonie d'immaculée conception, nos Athéniens").
11 *Menexenus* 237d–238a.
12 *Bibliotheca* III 14.2.

on Greek soil so that each may receive a share of selected honors. It is at this time that the immortals become *poliades*, that is to say, principal divinities of a territory or a city, a *polis*. This results in challenges, exchanges, compromises. And in Attica, or rather, "Cecropia" (?), there it is, reigning over a few natives, the first living being to be called autochthonous and whose name is Cecrops, a hybrid figure, half snake, half human. Then along comes a god, the first to want sovereignty over the land and city of Cecrops: Poseidon. He very properly carries a trident, plants it in the middle of the Acropolis, and out gushes a little sea that the local people today call Erectheis. Mythology says so, and so, one suspects, do others. After Poseidon comes Athena. She begins by asking Cecrops to serve as a witness, then causes an olive tree to sprout and grow, the tree that can still be seen today in the place called Pandroseion. Which of the two candidates will be victorious over the other? Zeus, the king of the gods, appoints a jury, made up of gods, the Twelve. Elsewhere, as at Argos, the members will be autochthons. After they have deliberated, Cecropia is given to Athena. The reason: Cecrops testified that Athena was first and planted the olive tree. No argument. Still, Poseidon too made a gift to Cecropia; the little sea, that symbol of maritime wealth and power. The sea god feels that he has been duped. Should he get Cecrops to witness that he was the first to demonstrate his power? Athena, arriving after Poseidon, seems to act as part of a jury about to render its verdict. Poseidon is vastly irritated. Salt water inundates the land of Cecrops that will soon become the city of Athens.

It is murmured that Poseidon has once more been evicted. But history does not stop there. It continues under the reign of Erechtheus. Euripides takes this as the plot of his play called *Erechtheus*.[13] Poseidon returns for round two, by way of Eleusis, where his son Eumolpos, the Tuneful Singer, is king. War breaks out between the Athenians of Erechtheus and the Thracians associated with Eumolpos and Poseidon—a real war between Athena's clan and Poseidon's. The city of Athens is in great danger. An oracle, coming post-haste from Delphi, announces that the blood of Erechtheus must run so that Athens can be saved. One of the daughters of the royal autochthon must have her throat cut, either on the altar of Persephone or else in honor of the Earth, of Gaia who thirsts for the blood of her children. It is Praxithea, the strong woman of Athens who will force her husband, Erechtheus, to spill the pure, necessary blood. Soon Praxithea will be consecrated Athena's priestess for life. Previously, it seems, Poseidon, furious at having witnessed the death of his son Eumolpos, had precipitated himself on Erechtheus and had buried him

---

13 Euripides *Fragments* (Jouan and Van Looy 2000), *Erechthée* fr. 13–14.

in a deep, open crevice in the center of the Acropolis, at the exact spot where between 421 and 420 BCE the Erechtheum will be raised. The very place, too, where Poseidon, arriving first, caused the little sea to spurt up. The legitimate autochthon then reigning over Athens is thus violently entombed in the earth from which, according to tradition, he was born. The temple-sanctuary called the Erechtheum thenceforth belongs to the god who had laid a prior claim to Attica. Poseidon is worshipped there under the name of Poseidon-Erechtheus, the murderer bearing the name of his victim.

And now, the god who had offered the sea to the native sons of Attica is coupled with Athena at the summit of the Acropolis. One family (*genos*), called the Eteoboutades, will inherit and share among themselves all the priestly functions for Poseidon-Erechtheus and Athena Polias. Erechtheus, already evoked in the *Iliad* as born of the earth, receives his offerings and sacrificial victims on the altar of Poseidon, who thus offers his hospitality to Athena's protégé. In an Athens exalted by the idea of its pure autochthony, it is noteworthy that the dead, those who died in the war, do not make for the kinds of good ancestors or illustrious predecessors that Barrès's nation demands. When all is said and done, the only illustrious dead man in this mythology written between 450 and 340 BCE is Erechtheus, shoved into his native soil by the power of Poseidon, the god of bedrock and unshakable foundations, at least when Athena's accomplice is not in a seismic humor. At the heart of the Erechtheum, Erechtheus the Firstborn signifies the rooting of the Athenians, whose autochthony is thus solidly planted. So autochthony, we see, can be founded. Without the help of Poseidon there is no truly rooted Athenian.

We should not, then, let ourselves be hoodwinked by the Athenians in that short time between the first funeral orations and the last. These speeches pass over in silence not only the founding role of Poseidon but also the series of political foundations in Athens; from Solon, so careful to make sure the laws, the *thesmoi* of communal life, would last, right up to Cleisthenes, who refounded the political field, fashioning it on the colonial model familiar to so many Greek cities. The navel-gazing of the Athenians seems to have fascinated the moderns to such an extent that most of them have not understood that foundation and autochthony have to be looked at together. Without a doubt, a comparative inquiry conducted together by historians and anthropologists on the question of creating a territory would allow us to put into more direct perspective (on one hand) the modalities of founding, beginning, creating, and (on the other) ways of being born of the earth, of growing in a furrow, or, as in certain Amerindian societies, of having the earth cling to the soles of one's feet in a territory that has no name, no distinguishing marks, no tombs, and no fixed sites.

Nothing is commoner in Greece or elsewhere than to proclaim oneself an autochthon. Every village has its first man; some, like the Arcadians, know with certainty that the first living being made his appearance even before the moon appeared in a sky dominated by the sun alone. In remote antiquity, Thebes, as famous as Troy, was alive with stories about its foundations— which also constitute its autochthony.[14] Being born of the earth and founding are, in effect, closely associated in the city of Cadmus, which is also one of those shared by two great gods, Apollo and Dionysus. Cadmus, the founder, sets out from Delphi. The Apollonian oracle enjoins him to follow an animal, future victim for the first sacrifice: its throat will be cut on the spot where it collapses exhausted on a site chosen by Apollo. Before the blood, which will soon flow, there is water. The search for the water necessary for the sacrifice sets in motion the process of founding. In the case of the future Thebes, the site is strongly marked by one already there. Apollo knows this not only through his omniscience but also by intentionality. First there is Ares, god of violence in warfare, the *purphoros* ready to burn Oedipus and his sons. Ares has copulated with a haughty Fury called Tilphousa, a power of resentment and vengeance, born of the Earth, of Gaia, when she received from emasculated Uranus the drops of blood from which also sprang the Giants and the Furies. The epichoric water is lodged in the deadly folds of the serpent born of Ares and Tilphousa. Murders and defilements are present at the origin of Thebes, for Ares' dragon kills the men who are searching for water. He in turn is killed by Cadmus, the first defilement marking Cadmus the founder. His exile will do nothing to purify him. The earth is ready for the second act: the dragon's teeth sown, on Ares' advice, in the furrows of Gaia, will cause to spring up from the earth new giants, men fully armed. The sown men, the Spartoi, wait only for a signal, rashly given by Cadmus, to kill and cut one another to bits. Where do we find autochthony in this? Ares, the already-there, bears the title of *Palaichthôn*, the 'one born of the soil,' the rooted. As for the Spartoi, the sown of Thebes, they are said to be born of the earth. Their blood, already impure, waters the furrows. So Gaia receives the blood of the firstborn sown at the same time as she drinks the red libation of the first victim sacrificed in the Apollonian manner of the god Archegetes-Founder. The god of Delphi is never absent from the history of Thebes. It is he who finishes off the story of Oedipus, crime upon crime; it is he who is waiting, watching at his gate, the

14 Cf. Detienne 2000a:61–120 ("Naître impur à Thèbes").

seventh, when the two brothers born of the incest of son and mother murder one another.

So, what kind of city can come into being because of leftovers, those five men who survive the bloodbath which inaugurates the city of Cadmus? It will have to be a city that can never pride itself on its origins as does Athens, a city tragically torn between founding and autochthony. This is what is shown in *Oedipus Rex*, the end of the *Bacchae,* and also the *Phoenician Women*. In this last tragedy, saving Thebes requires that the blood of an autochthon should be spilled. Ares thirsts for blood, again and again, never-endingly. The god of Delphi and Thebes, Apollo, lets it be known that the god of war and original defilement demands as victim a pure-blood descendant of the race of the Spartoi on both his mother's side and through the male line. Menoeceus, the chosen one, is to kill himself, cut his throat, and spill his blood near the gates of Thebes so the city may then be solidly rooted. This picks up the theme of the gates or fortifications of Athens, which required, in the reign of Erechtheus, autochthonous blood, whether that of Agraulos or another woman born of the very earth of the Firstborn.

Seen from Thebes, the Athenian vanity of being the only true autochthons is both laughable and ridiculous. In the city of Cadmus and Oedipus, foundation and autochthony commingle under the dominant sign of defilement, of the impurity of spilled blood, and of insatiable revenge. Since the recent discovery of the bronze tablets of Selinous, we know that in Greece it is possible to have pure ancestors, and others who are impure but who can be purified.[15] Those Theban ancestors are deeply impure, and everything shows us that nothing and nobody can wash away a defilement which is born again of itself like the olive tree on the Acropolis. An autochthony of blood and death.

One is not old-stock French as one is an autochthonous Theban or Athenian. There are ten or twenty ways of founding one's autochthony. Just let the circle of inquiry be widened to include historians and anthropologists. But, one might ask, what is the use of comparing cultural experiences dispersed through time and space? I would reply without hesitation: in analyzing some experiences in the light of others, we provide ourselves with the means of better understanding those murderous throbbings of identity which pulse in the human societies of yesterday, today, and tomorrow.

---

15 Jameson, Jordan, and Kotansky 1993, and comments in Georgoudi 2001.

2

Being Born Impure in the City of Cadmus and Oedipus*

HUMAN VANITY IS A LIMITLESSLY entertaining subject, and if I have chosen to ask myself, "how can one be autochthonous?" it is because the pride of being rooted or of believing oneself to be of cleansed blood is a sickness as laughable as chicken pox. Its consequences, however, can be the death of thousands, or millions, of innocent people. In my opinion, it is not a futile exercise to put groups of natives, proud of their roots, in perspective—yes, by comparing them with each other. For example, I find interesting the idea of comparing the invention of autochthony in Athens, which took place around 450 CE, and that of old-stock French from Maurice Barrès to the Far Right of the 1980s and into the present. Two myth-ideologies, one of which valorizes being born in an exceptional land, thus guaranteeing purity and authorizing the disdain of all immigrants, while the other places importance in tracing one's roots and one's dead all the way back to the prehistoric period. Athenian vanity is founded on the repetitive discourse of funeral orations, while the pride of the old-stock French feeds on the continuity of the history of France and of stories about France produced by historians.

"The Earth and the Dead"—this is the slogan created by Barrès and reused by the Vichy government before Jean-Marie Le Pen and the National Front. Why not the "Blood and Soil," the *Blut und Boden* that worked so well in Germany during the 1930s? There was a mythology of blood in France in the middle of the seventeenth century.[1] It lasted a little more than a century and then disappeared without leaving a trace, not even in the work of Gobineau. I mean the nobility that claimed and craved to be of "cleansed blood." (Our

---

* This chapter is a revision of an article published in *Arion* 10.3 (Winter 2003) 35–47.
1 Cf. Devyver 1973.

worries about blood are not over.) Nobility was threatened in its privileges. It cried out its horror of contaminated blood: its ideologist, the Count of Boulainvilliers, showed that the nobles were the descendants of the Franks, therefore warriors who came from the forests of Germania and who, thanks to the excellence of their blood that was shed in war, dominated the serfs, Gallic peasants enslaved to the land. It was a noble blood that had to be cleansed, made more pure through alliances between nobles. The roots were abandoned to the *culs-terreux*, as we say in French, or people of the land. How, indeed, after the Six Days' War, could an old-stock Jew with roots in the land of Jerusalem be created in Israel when faced with the Bedouin nomad from Palestine?[2]

This is off the subject, but when I look at the traditions of Thebes, the city of Cadmus, I cannot help thinking of about Greater Serbia and the pure-blooded Serbs, purifying Kosovo of its impure Albanians. Thebes–Athens: I do not intend to play with the *anti-* (Thebes, anti-Athens, or reciprocally). I would rather come back to the contrast between *being autochthonous* and *to found, implant, establish.* Common sense—and it awakens us every morning—seems to make a strong distinction between being born, growing up, sprouting up out of one's soil and one's land, always the same, on the one hand, and, on the other, coming from the exterior, arriving from abroad, to create a village, a town, or a city. Between the eighth and the fourth centuries BCE, the Greeks founded in this manner tens, maybe hundreds, of cities in Magna Graecia, in Sicily, and on the banks of the Black Sea. In the eyes of the pure autochthons from Athens, those who emerge in the middle of the fifth century and who, fortunately, are sneered at by Euripides and a few others, all of the cities of Greece, including the Arcadians or the Argives, are made up of immigrants, people who have come from who knows where and who cannot claim to be autochthons like the children of Athena, and I might add, of Poseidon. Indeed, one has only to go back to the mythological history of Athens, following Euripides' account in his *Erechtheus*, in order to discover that autochthony must be founded—yes, dear Athenians, it has to be rooted, much the way Poseidon does when he pushes Erechtheus, the Born of the Land, straight into the rock of the Acropolis, under the Erechtheum, right where Poseidon-Erechtheus received official worship next to Athena Polias. Autochthony and foundation are combined in Athens. In Thebes, the two methods intertwine differently and in a way that puts blood in the foreground, blood shed and to be shed. If we lend importance to

2 Cf. Attias and Benbassa 2001.

the past, at Athens it appears to be in short supply. Thucydides is harsh when he evokes the olden days of Attica:[3] stones without a past, a land good for fugitives and exiles; and, as a matter of fact, Solon naturalized anything that passed within proximity.[4] All the while, Thebes, as early as the eighth century, received its noble pedigree from a vast epic, the *Thebaid*, that tells of the great deeds of the City of Seven Gates brought up in the *Odyssey*. Thebes is the only Greek city that can rival Troy, the well founded, the city of impregnable walls. In recent years, archeologists have found the correspondence of Cadmus or, at least, the Mycenaean archives of his palace. There is even evidence of a lyre player, a *lurastês*, undoubtedly a storyteller like Demodocus or Homer, in the service of the Theban Alcinous.[5]

But the mythology of Thebes never stops being told and retold, between epic songs and tragedies, not to mention the very active logographers from the fifth century. Thebes is founded not once, but twice. This is where the polytheistic regime is imposed, feeding the tales of the mythographers and the plots of tragedy. Thebes is rich in gods, and its beginnings are marked with divine acts. The gods are there and will not cease to be present and inhabit the city from one generation to the next. Two of them are greater than the others and are often accomplices: one is Apollo, the other Dionysus. They interact, they meet by chance, they know each other, and they recognize each other at leisure. Characteristic trait: they are gods who have to deal with evil and with defilement. Let us leave the Dionysus of Cadmus with his impurity on the side of Agave and Pentheus, and follow step by step the deeds of Apollo. He is the great god of the *Daphnêphoria*, Thebes' major celebration in honor of the Laurel Bearer. In Thebes, Apollo sits as an oracular god in his pied-à-terre in Ismenion.[6] This great god is not without ambiguity: we know him, perhaps, knife in hand. There is Apollo the Butcher. On his altar in Delphi, he slit the throat of his privileged enemy in order to give some spark to the Day of Hospitality, the *Theoxenia*.[7]

Born in Delos, Apollo then leaves to firmly establish in Delphi the sanctuary from which any and all foundations will henceforth be instituted. Apollo is a walking god. He crosses a good part of Greece. And he begins to act quite

---

3 Thucydides 1.2.5–6.
4 Cf. Ruzé 2000.
5 Bernardini 2000.
6 Vian 1963.
7 Detienne 1998a:186–194.

strangely as he nears Thebes. First, Thebes goes unmentioned in the version of the *Homeric Hymn*. A huge untamed forest is raised in its spot. The city will rise up, but later, after Delphi; and Apollo continues on his way.[8] Another vision is found in the *Hymn to Delos* by Callimachus, poet of the Alexandrian library. His Apollo, only seven months along, travels in the womb of Leto, his fleeing mother. The anger of Hera, the legitimate wife, forces them to flee forever further away in the night. As they near the city of Cadmus, Apollo starts to move, he vituperates and threatens Thebes—the Thebes that is to come. Apollo insults her. He is telling Thebes to run, to run from the inescapable arrows. What is this all about? Apollo of only seven months already sees his bow drenched in blood, the blood shed by a mother with an impudent tongue. This primordial mother is, assuredly, Niobe, another autochthonous woman in the landscape of Thebes; Niobe, proud, too proud of having given birth to six sons and six daughters, and who commiserates with Leto and her twins: two children? Is that all? Apollo declares loudly in the night that he does not want to be born in Thebes. He makes it very clear: "Pure (*euagês*), I only want to be in the hearts of those who are pure, (*euagês*)."[9] Strange, as if even before the arrival of Cadmus and his foundation for autochthons, there is contamination in the air, a stain that is "already there"!

Examined closely and far from the academies, Apollo is a somber and violent god: the pure exile from heaven, as he was called by Aeschylus, who knew of his murders in Olympus and elsewhere.[10] It is in Delphi that the history of Thebes is set in motion, and the comings and goings between Thebes and the sanctuary of Apollo will never cease. It all starts in the most ordinary way. One consultation day, a certain Cadmus comes before the Pythia. His sister is nowhere to be found—her name is Europa. Apollo tells him not to worry: Cadmus has more important things to do. Pythia enjoins him in carefully chosen hexameters to leave and to found a city, the city of Cadmus. An animal guide awaits him at the threshold of the oracle. All he needs to do is follow it and sacrifice the offered victim at the place where it collapses from exhaustion. Cadmus follows the instructions. He does not know what lies ahead for him. Apollo, however, knows exactly where he is going to cross the path of Dionysus. But another of Apollo's accomplices is already there.[11]

---

8 Ibid., 22–23.
9 Callimachus *Hymn to Delos* 86–98 Gigante.
10 Detienne 1998a:175–234.
11 Vian 1963:76–113.

Performing a sacrifice is easy to talk about, but the ritual comes with certain obligations. Where is he to find the water for the preparatory libation? A search for water ensues. There is an abundance of it at the fountain of Ares. Yes, Ares, the god of war, or better yet, of warlike fury. And, as a matter of fact, he is settled there.[12] Attracted, they say, by the charms of an Erinys: Tilphousa, born of Gaia, a sort of "autochthonous" power, born of the land, the very cosmogonic land.[13] The land that received on its face, with an immense joy, the drops of blood from Uranus, when the heavens were finally emasculated by Cronus' scythe, the white metal of which had been conceived by the land itself in its crafty entrails. There is here something of a first evil. From these drops of blood will be born the powers of resentment, the family of the Erinyes and, next to them, the Giants, beings devoted to unlimited war. Ares, in his desire to settle, could not have found a better place.[14]

Here is the site chosen by Apollo of Delphi for Cadmus who is wondering what has happened to his sister Europa. Apollo knows what will happen in the future Thebes; he knows its past, its present, and its future. Apollo is there to take care of Cadmus' city and his progeny—the rest, in short. The water of the fountain is clear. One needs only to draw it from the coils of a serpent, a serpent all the less likable for being born from the love of Ares and Erinys. Seeing that two, and then four, of his companions fail to return, Cadmus becomes angry. He slits the throat of the dragon at the fountain without suspecting that here, at the site of the future city, he is shedding the blood of the son of Ares and Erinys, two powers heavy with resentment and experts in indelible stains. Ares will never cease to recall this first bloodshed, to each generation and through the children, from the sons of Cadmus to Oedipus and to Menoeceus, Creon's son.

The second act can begin with Earth (*Gaia*) a polymorphous power in the pantheon of Thebes. In the meantime, Cadmus, back with the lustral water, sacrifices the guide animal, undoubtedly invoking, like all founders, Apollo *Arkhêgetês*, the god who accompanied him to found the promised city. The warrior dragon had a beautiful set of teeth. On Ares' advice, Cadmus sets about sowing them. They hardly touch the furrows in the ground before a terrible crop of men at arms sprouts up, cousins of the Giants and, like them, devoted to unlimited war. Having barely brushed off the soil, the Sown,

---

12 Detienne 2003a:80
13 Vian 1963:107–108.
14 Hesiod *Theogony* 173–187. Cf. Detienne 1998a:163–167.

who are the *Spartoi* in Greek, throw themselves at each others' throats. A horrible massacre ensues. The only survivors are five Spartoi, Cadmus' first companions, who will be consecrated citizens of Thebes.[15] Let us stop here for an instant. If the founder sent by Apollo to a more or less untamed land is of an easily recognized type, what characterizes autochthony on Theban ground? First, there is what is signified by Ares, called *Palaichthon*, the Quite-Anciently-of-the-Earth, the Earth where the Erinys sprouts up from a drop of Uranian blood.[16] The Erinys Tilphousa is even more local in provenance than her lover. Next, there are the true natives, the Sown, authentically born of the land. Their blood, impure from the beginning, waters the furrows of Gaia who, on this day of foundation mixed with autochthony, drinks joyfully of the red juice from the first fruits of the city of Cadmus' Firstborn.

To be born impure: we quickly see what this signifies in the city of Laius and Oedipus. The children born of the land of Cadmus kill each other, in murder after murder for generations, a stain that is unendingly revived. Who leads the game being played in Thebes? Who has been conducting it since the appearance of Cadmus? A great god, alone, even if his accomplices are present: he whom one of his most famous victims will designate by screaming, "It's he, it is he who did it."[17] The tragedies made of Theban matter constantly bring to mind the powerfully maleficent role played by the Master of Delphi.[18] Some evidence, in the form of texts: Sophocles' *Oedipus Rex*. The text by Aeschylus has been lost, unless some undergraduate copied it and his master threw it away in a garbage can of Fayum. At the opening of the Sophoclean tragedy there is a plague (*loimos*) that strikes the earth and the women with sterility. It is a consuming fire, it is even a god called Fire Bearer (*Purphoros*).[19] The chorus will soon say: "It's Ares!"[20] What can be done? Invoke Apollo. Is he not the god of medicine, Apollo *Iatros*, the god of Thebes, the one who knows so well how to get rid of plagues?[21] Very quickly, in the same chorus, the anxiety peaks, the type of anxiety that is caused by the appearance of a plague, a sickness of the earth and of an entire city (a *loimos*, a *nosos*). Is there some debt (*chreos*) to be paid? An old debt?[22] Apollo's blind

---

15 Vian 1963:106–113.
16 Aeschylus *Seven Against Thebes* 104. Cf. Vian 1963:108.
17 Sophocles *Oedipus Rex* 377.
18 Detienne 2003a:84–87.
19 *Oedipus Rex* 27–28.
20 *Oedipus Rex* 190–192.
21 Detienne 1998a:208, 330, 344.
22 *Oedipus Rex* 155–157.

prophet, Teiresias, comes onstage. Upset by Oedipus—Freud would say that this Oedipus character has problems—he throws out the truth like a thunderbolt, the truth that no one can bear: the impurity that you are looking for, the stain that you have cursed, it is you, Oedipus, and Apollo is here, he is ready to carry out what must be done (*ekpraksai*, he is in full *praxis*).[23]

The chorus oscillates between anxiety and hope. Anguish first, especially as it addresses a prayer to the Apollo who dropped the mask of the Good Doctor to pick up that of the armed god full of fire equal to the initial plague, denoted by Ares in the first scene. This time it is the Erinyes who follow in Apollo's footsteps.[24] We are right to say that the tragic poets are full of mythology, that they know all of the configurations. The time has come for Oedipus to understand that he is "criminal" (*kakos*), and as the result of the act of a cruel, savage (*ômos*, a quality of Dionysus when he lets loose) god. Who is, then, this god? Oedipus will finally give him his true name, Jocasta has hung herself, he has just gouged out his eyes: "The one who adds crime upon crime, the god who is leading all of this to its end, is Apollo!"[25] Teiresias had said it! Too soon, too fast. Yes, it is a performance by Apollo, the god who cried out in the night to Leto that he was pure (*euagês*) and did not want anything to do with Thebes. Really?

Is this enough for Cadmus' Thebes? Everything must continue. Oedipus is not, he cannot be, the so-called scapegoat, a *pharmakos*—ambiguous of course, but whose limits Apollo knows better than anybody: he, the official god of the Thargelia, the feast with *pharmakoi*.[26] Ares, the god of Thebes who is so close to him, is already coming back onstage. This time, it is in the *Phoenician Women*. (Euripides is a great mythologist.) At the opening, there is "Ares' resentment" (*palaia mênimata*), explicit, displayed. Cadmus killed one of his sons, the blood-thirsty and murderous serpent. Cadmus shed Ares' blood, and old murders awaken new murders. Polynices believes that he is invoking the Apollo of his house, the god of roads, Apollo *Aguieus*—like Jocasta on the morning of the day that everything is going to change—and it is the Apollo of the Labdacids that responds, the one who, by means of Teiresias' oracles and exhaustion, demands from Thebes, supposedly in order to save her, that the blood of a child born from the mouth of the dragon be shed. They must give to the earth the red life of a pure descendant of the Spartoi: through the mother as well as through the

23 *Oedipus Rex* 350–353, 377.
24 *Oedipus Rex* 469–472.
25 *Oedipus Rex* 1327–1330.
26 Detienne 2003a:88–90.

males. He is there; it is the son of Creon, slitting his own throat in libation to the forever-thirsty earth of Thebes. Teiresias says it again so as to be clearly understood: it is the consequence of the old resentments conceived by Ares against Cadmus. There is no salvation for Thebes. Menoeceus' blood has barely emptied itself into the earth when the sons of Oedipus, still in the *Phoenician Women*, kill each other, when Jocasta puts an end to her deplorable days, and when Oedipus, more and more stained, goes off toward other adventures.[27]

The Theban evil is ineradicable. The race of the Spartoi, doubly impure autochthons, appears like a "splendid disgrace" (*oneidos*), a superb insult, says the chorus of *Oedipus Rex*, made by Cadmus to the land of Thebes.[28] Here is, therefore, a beautiful original impurity that is transmitted across Cadmus' entire lineage, polluting Cadmus himself, Laius, Oedipus, Oedipus' children, and the descendants of Creon. "To be born impure," how can we understand it if we do not want to make Thebes into nothing more than a cursed city? I would like to insist on what "ineradicable" means for a stain; and in a like manner to examine certain aspects of the specific relation between a god like Apollo and the question of evil.

Pure, impure, the contexts are numerous, and at different times in the history of a single culture, several types of pollution must be hypothesized. I am aiming specifically at the complexity of the configurations that link the impure to the pure. My goal is not to do comparative studies in a field that certainly has no need for it. I merely need to make a rapid incursion into societies of western Africa, thanks to the complicity of ethnologists who have helped me to clear what they call the "fields of stain."[29] On the Ivory Coast, among the *Senoufo*, there seems to be a strong tie between a type of stain and asocial space. This tie is established by a power, sometimes anonymous, that sanctions the stain that occurs within its jurisdiction. What stain? There is murder, but also the stain of sex, that designates a *social space* at the limits of which its effects spread and make themselves felt. All those who belong to this social space are thus affected, contaminated by the effects of the stain of one individual. More specifically, what is this social space? It can be that of an altar, said to be an altar of the earth, all of whose members are affected. A stain, in this case, indicates that a segment of space is suddenly polluted. Let us go more quickly: a field of stain seems to be thought of like a body, a body-

---

27 Ibid., 92–97.
28 Euripides *Phoenician Women* 821.
29 Detienne 2003a:97–100; also Cartry and Detienne 1996.

space. It is a full and closed body that the murder (or the stain of sex) comes to injure in the form of a first cut. *How* does the ritual of purification proceed? Pure-impure make a pair, I insist. The ritual, the object of our reflection in the context of the *Senoufo*, does not aim to purify the agent of the stain, but to redefine the limits of the social space that has been affected, wounded. The procedure set in motion seeks to encase the stain, to encyst it in the interior of the wounded social space. Very specifically, to set the stain on an altar made for this purpose: a so-called altar of murder, for example, with murderers gathered in a fraternity to serve it. In a context that we would call Greek, in general, the murderer and his stain must be expulsed, chased out. The African example that I chose for its *dissonant* character leads us to valorize the stain, in particular that of murder. There are societies like that: masculine initiation includes murder. So be it. It is a choice, an orientation. In other societies, the stain does not affect a territory or a body-space: it touches people and statutes exclusively. In Vedic India, according to interpreters like Charles Malamoud, to get rid of a stain that affects a person or a statute, it is placed in the earth. The earth is a garbage can. My, how bizarre these people are!

And what about the Greeks, or at least certain Greeks some of whose representations, practices, and rituals are known to us? What is a *miasma*, an *agos*?[30] These are two Greek words for stain; and when thinking of Thebes, we must immediately add the semantic field of plague (*loimos, limos, nosos*), of the so-called bubonic plague, of those diseases of the entire social body (children, fruits of the earth, herd animals).

Here I will limit myself to just a few observations: there are social spaces where the stain is transmissible. (I keep the stain of spilled blood, leaving aside that of sex: incest of the second degree does not stain—and, for a certain Oedipus, this could be of interest.) Infection, contagion, contamination—there are implicit models, explicit theories, that one can expect to find in certain Greek cities where doctors mull over what we call epidemics, whereas rituals and purifiers are charged with the treatment of different types of stains.

Take the question of space, social places, affected by the impure, the major stain, that of spilled blood. We know some of them quite well: the basins of lustral water and the entrances to public or consecrated places (agoras, meeting places, sanctuaries), banquet-room kraters. All altars and sanctuaries. These are the living parts of the urban social body; this is where the stain

---

30 Detienne 2003a:100–102.

infects the worst and the most quickly the entirety of the social body. So the murderer is prohibited from entering, is excluded from these social places, and is thus already in exile. And he will be totally exiled if he is found guilty. Very early on, Greek cities invented tribunals, and first for spilled blood. In cases of homicide, yes, not incest, it must be repeated.

And what about the stain over time?[31] This is something that directly concerns Thebes. We remember: the site of the future Thebes marked with blood, the blood that Apollo sees himself spilling while the god is still an embryo on his way to Delos. Yes, there are stains that are transmitted through time, across several generations; this is normal, without being commonplace. Aeschylus knows about it, and so do many others. These are stains that do not age; they are still young and alert. They "do not fade." The stain of the Atreids, the one that incessantly rejuvenates in the family of Thyestes and Atreus. The stain of Minyas' daughters who devoured their children under the effect of Dionysus and his vengeful madness: seventeen generations, according to the calculations made by Plutarch, who considers that it is not finished. We are in the domain of ancient resentments (*palaia mênimata*), of those violent and inextinguishable fits of anger born from an unforgettable murder. For example, the blood shed by Ares' son, or by the Firstborn of the land of Thebes who massacre each other.

One can be born, then, not "cursed" but impure "without knowing it," "without wanting it," inheriting, as the old Oedipus at Colonus would say, an ancient injury (*oneidos*), the *oneidos* inflicted on the land of Thebes by Cadmus.[32] (I would even say: more ancient than he—and I would look Apollo in the eyes, just for a second, just one). Yes, there are pure Ancestors, and others who are impure, stained (*miarai*). We have known for a long time the impurities, the stains, the so-called Genius Avengers (*Alastores*) who never forget, like the unforgetting (*mnêmones*) Erinyes. Yes, Ares' family, and I would say Apollo's too, in Thebes. Only recently, and thanks to the 1993 publication of the writing tablets of Selinous, we have come to know the Great-Grandfathers, impure, polluted; and others qualified as pure. These are the Ancestors, called *Tritopatores*. Were the pure Ancestors purified? This is quite probable. Whereas the impure Great-Grandfathers have not yet been, and the

31 Ibid., 102–104.
32 Sophocles *Oedipus at Colonus* 964–965, 966–968.

sacrifices that are offered to them "as to heroes" are reserved for "those for whom it is allowed" (*tois hosia*).[33]

It is in this context of stain transmitted through time, of ancestral and very ancient impurity, that we can try to understand what it means to "be born impure in Thebes." In Thebes, insofar as it is the city of Cadmus and Oedipus.

So, one last step remains: how can one be Theban? Son of a city that is rich in feats of war, those of the Aegeids who will be the masters of war for the Spartans; those of the victorious phalanxes of Epaminondas; and those of so many victors of the Isthmian, Pythian, and other games? Or perhaps Theban in the manner of Pindar who celebrates Dionysus, Heracles, Apollo, the warrior saints of the city of Cadmus; and who chooses to throw a cloak over all of the spilled blood, to forget . . . the unforgettable, the stain that goes so far back in time and that, as Laius' son says over and over, was orchestrated by Apollo. Unless the god of Delphi was himself lured into doing what he did, without wanting to and without knowing it. Should Leto's embryo plead guilty or not guilty? For the time being, we have a god who is intimately mixed up with the question of evil. He is not the only one, we must remember. It is a good question for those who like to contemplate the notions of blood and autochthony—cleansed blood, pure and impure blood, the Land, the Dead, and the Ancestors, of so many different colors.

---

33 See Jameson, Jordan, and Kotansky 1993.

PART II

Every God Is Plural

1

Experimenting in the Field of Polytheisms[*]

T HE DISCOVERY THAT GODS make good objects of research was not made by
contemporary anthropology. The very first anthropologists never failed
to recommend making an inventory of the various kinds of powers at
large in a village or scattered the length and breadth of a kingdom. However, by
the end of the nineteenth century, two generally shared beliefs were obstructing
the analysis of those vast groups of supernatural powers distributed among the
archaic societies and civilizations of history that were then held in the highest
esteem, such as—to give a random sample—China, India, and Greece. It would
seem that the first comparatists, from Tylor to Frazer, were convinced that the
stable, if not permanent, element in all cultures was ritual organized around a
single theme, with a whole structure of festivals and holy days in the calendar.
This justified the fascinated attention that they paid to ceremonies marking
turning points in the year or to the adventures of magic kings in Africa, in India,
and in classic civilizations ranging from Italy to Scandinavia.

At the same time the anthropologists, believing as they did that divine
entities come and go and reappear without reason, tended to share the
conviction that all the figures in this fluid and inconsistent supernatural
world needed to be explained separately, if they could lay claim to names
of their own and to individual characteristics. Throughout the nineteenth
century, both ethnology and the history of religions were preoccupied with
genesis and evolution. For partisans of animism, devotees of totemism, and
theorists of the elementary forms of religious life, representations of the
soul, different types of spirit, and the forms taken by superior entities all
provided viable approaches to the major question: namely, the origin and
development of the idea of the divine. In the field of Greek religion, far from
the inhabitants of Nigritia (whom President de Brosses encouraged to bear
witness to the idolatry and fetishism of original times), one philosopher

* Originally published in *Arion* 7.1 (Spring/Summer 1999) 127–149.

seems to have pointed the way forward: Hegel recognized the existence of a pantheon peopled with gods who lived together, each with a personal life, and with conflicting passions and interests. The gods of Olympus ceased to be cold allegories, each set upon a pedestal. Each one became a signifying form, but the "polytheistic" (from the Greek *polutheos*) world seemed impossible to organize into a systematically articulated whole.[1] Then Olympus was discovered through Homer's mirror, and those who wrote its history, such as Creuzer and Welcker, were more concerned to discover an intuition of the absolute[2] among the gods of Greece than to explore the different ways in which they were grouped together that had been observed by Pausanias in his description of Greece at the time of Hadrian.

In the early years of the twentieth century, the division deepened between, on the one hand, the "gods of crossroads" such as those of Nigritia and, on the other, the great gods of a polytheism that had been restored to its erstwhile paradigmatic state, that is to say confined to Greek culture shut in upon itself and once more the private domain of its own preferred historians, who showed no interest in any comparative reflection on the polytheistic groups of either yesterday or today. Between the 1920s and the 1940s, the preserve of the Greek gods was the scene of a clash between positivist historians and spiritual interpreters. On the one hand, Martin P. Nilsson, with his flawless erudition, tackled the divine powers from the vantage point of common sense and on a solid no-nonsense basis that enabled him to identify simple representations that researches into history and the imaginary were later to deck out with multiple, many-faceted figures. On the other hand, Walter F. Otto, with his intelligent hermeneutics, tried to show that each god signified a particular sphere of existence, an exemplary experience of mankind "present in the world." Those two approaches were not without their respective merits, but both were equally indifferent to the actual nature of polytheism: a complex system of relations between a variety of supernatural powers and entities.

It was with Georges Dumézil and under his influence that, in the 1960s, historians and anthropologists began to take an interest in polytheistic groups on their own account, in how those systems of gods were organized, and in the various ways that societies such as Greece, Rome, and India saw themselves through those religious entities. Dumézil replaced the historico-genetic approach, which was dominant in his day, by a "structural" analysis that concentrated on complementarities, oppositions, hierarchies, and complexes

---

1 See Detienne 1984.
2 Bravo 1988.

of relations. After twenty years spent analyzing the configurations of gods and microsystems dispersed throughout his own preferred field of research, namely the Indo-European domain, Georges Dumézil began to exert a major influence on scholars resolved to take the gods seriously, whether in the Caucasus,[3] in Greece,[4] or in India.[5]

It is worth pausing to reflect on this: the gods that Dumézil discovered or helped others to discover played an essential role in the *comparative* (and *experimental*) study of the "religions of the Indo-European peoples." Indeed that was more or less the name given to the department of studies at the *École Pratique des Hautes Études* (*Sciences Religieuses*) where Dumézil was to work for thirty years. The old subject of "comparative mythology" that he had chosen in 1935 was eclipsed in 1945 and by 1948 had given way to "Indo-European civilization," this time at the Collège de France and in other scholarly circles.[6] The starting point for Dumézil's intellectual undertaking was gods who were interactive, gods in groups, collections of divine powers. The old "comparative mythology" had sought to apprehend their essence and etymology on the basis of linguistic equations. The new comparative method, established in the domain of Indo-European studies, was, for its part, primarily interested in the order in which they were listed, the hierarchical relations between them, and the forms of opposition or complementarity that made it possible to explore "theological" data such as the precapitoline triad formed by Jupiter, Mars, and Quirinus; the triad of Upsala gods (Odhinn, Thôrr, Frejya); the list of the Âditya in ancient India; and that of the Entities (the *Amasa Spanta*) of Zoroastrianism in ancient Iran.[7] These were complex but primary data that established what Dumézil was to call "the fact of structure,"[8] and thereby facilitated access to the "ultrahistory" of Indo-European civilization, which was now to be enriched by interconnected groups of concepts detected from a strictly structured common vocabulary that formed the framework for a system of thought in which "asterisks" proliferated and which was invariably proto- if not pre-historic.

Analysts of polytheistic groups unrestricted by Indo-European constraints were to continue to adhere to a number of the principles on which Dumézil's inquiries were based. The first, already mentioned above, was to pay attention to the structures that were immediately apparent in many polythe-

---

3 See G. Charachidzè 1968.
4 See Vernant 1983:127–176.
5 See Dumont 1957:396–403.
6 See Dumézil 1968 :165–167.
7 See Dumézil 1952 and 1977.
8 See e.g. Dumézil 1973:10–16.

isms; altars devoted to a plurality of gods; sanctuaries consecrated to several gods at once; festivals and rituals that associated now two deities brought together for a particular occasion, now two different aspects of a single power; aspects that were contrasted in various ways—by their respective modes of sacrifice, for example. The polytheistic societies of both yesterday and today manifest a wealth of collections of deities, in circumstantial or recurrent groupings, and in monumental or ephemeral configurations. The "already-structural" (to respect Dumézil's terminology) is the raw material for analysts, who will gather what they will from it, before embarking on their own hunt. The "structures" are there; you simply need to take care not to trample them underfoot, for with a modicum of skill those "savage thoughts" can be deciphered, along with what they signify or are beginning to signify.

The second principle, which stems from the first but makes it possible to circumvent the limitations of the trifunctional framework so necessary to Dumézilian thought, is that no god can be defined in static terms. The analyst's task is to identify the entire range of positions occupied by a deity within a polytheistic group. Alongside what is made "clearly manifest"[9] about the gods and their actions—which the skills of ultrahistory aim to fasten on first and foremost in every culture—the analyst needs to identify all the forms of association and contrast that the culture experiments with, even implicitly. In the process, the analyst, believing that it is necessary to study the gods in relation to one another, will strive to define their respective limits and to establish the boundaries between their respective fields of action. The assumption common to much new research carried out or authorized by Dumézil (it must be emphasized) was that the surest validation for an analysis of the relations between gods or the definition of the field of action peculiar to a divine power would stem from some native statement, particularly one of a theological nature: a statement produced by the polytheistic theologians who were, in fact, frequently the "administrators of memory" and who, down through the ages, transmitted not only the most conscious beliefs but also, along with those, all that was abandoned to the historical subconscious of the language and the civilization that that language conveyed.

The last principle, sketched in by Dumézil in 1949 and confirmed in 1966, was at once more innovative and harder to put into practice.[10] More innovative, because it introduced an important distinction between a god's field of action and that god's mode of action. The field of action of divine power

---

9 See e.g. Dumézil 1954:78.
10 Dumézil 1949:1 and 1966:179, 229.

encompassed the places and occasions where gods offered their services; and some deities, led on, as it were, by the overdevelopment of the "function" to which they were linked, found themselves intervening in domains very distant from what appeared to be their basic province. So the thing to do is to discover "not *where* a god intervenes but *how* the god does." To define a god's modes of action is thus to move beyond the points at which the god intervenes, beyond the scenes in which the god appears, and to seek to establish "a constant manner and constant means of action." The mode of action must be precise and specific to each god. This was a very innovative principle when applied to experimental practices that Dumézil envisaged very early on but which, once applied, clashed with the fundamental structures of the Indo-European civilization that he was seeking to understand, that is to say, with the three functions and the whole pattern of tripartition. For Dumézil, a function was synonymous with activity, social activity, the activities of men in society, those who wielded power, those who waged war, and those who produced goods and food. The most important gods were those who presided, alone or in couples, over the major functions, and were active in that way: they were agents, and very busy ones too. Dumézil frequently calls them "patron-gods" (the bosses). Doggedly, he analyses the interrelations of these divine figures from one function to another, always mindful of the different "aspects" of a particular function, but more inclined to dwell on the basic characteristics of the deities who were "patron-gods," while leaving aside those who performed "lateral and accessory" services.

Let us pause to reflect on that formula: "the basic characteristics of the patron-gods."[11] It echoes what the Greeks, from Homer down to Herodotus, thought, and indeed said, about their gods: namely, that each of the divine powers had been allotted a *timê*, a particular field of action that was the god's prerogative and that was limited by the conditions of the allotment. The most famous distribution was that organized by the new king of the gods following his victory over the Titans. Each god and each goddess was allotted what the *Iliad* calls *erga*, that is to say tasks, work to do, activities: tasks of which both the gods and men show themselves to be very much aware when they talk about them among themselves. In book 5 of the *Iliad*, Aphrodite flies to the aid of Aeneas, who is in deadly peril as he confronts Diomedes who, for his part, immediately recognizes Aphrodite and relishes using his physical strength to hurt her, "knowing that she is a god without strength (*analkis*), and not one of the goddesses who have mastery in men's battles, not Athena or Enyo, the

11 Dumézil 1949:78.

sacker of cities."[12] Aphrodite is wounded and her blood, or rather *ikhôr*, begins to flow. Fainting, she manages to reach her lover-brother Ares, and begs him to spirit her away immediately. Zeus consoles her, at the same time tapping her on the cheek and reminding her that she is not a deity who has been allotted the works of war. "War's work, my child, is not your province. No, you busy yourself with marriage and the work of love." The two "functions" or domains of activity are distinct, separate, carefully delimited—or seem to be. Yet, as is quite clear to any observer of Greek polytheism, in "marriage and the work of love" Aphrodite does not operate alone: Hera, known as the Accomplished One (*teleia*) is also active there, together with Zeus, who is likewise *teleos*; and the sensual Charites are present, along with the Seasons, the *Hôrai*, as are Hermes and Artemis. Similarly, the "works of war" mobilize not only—obviously enough—Athena and Ares, but also Enyô and Enyalios, not to mention the couple formed by Ares and Aphrodite who, in Argos and possibly also in Crete, were stationed at the gates of war. Zeus is as much aware of all this as is Diomedes, even though he tells Aphrodite that where the works of war are concerned, it is Athena and the ardent Ares who are constantly vigilant. Equally aware are the other powers who are deliberately kept out of it at this point: it would have been inappropriate for the Aphrodite of Ares to confront Diomedes and Athena.

According to this model—and what a model it is, homemade, and (what is more) by Homer!—there are, on the one hand, respective domains assigned to the great gods, all with their limits: one god must not encroach on the domain of another; and woe betide any mortal who forgets to acknowledge the preserve of the appropriate deity on setting out to sea, deciding to marry, or going off to war. On the other hand, each of these "great domains"—or "functions," as Dumézil called them—is crossed by a whole series of powers or, in some cases, shared by a large number of gods, each of whom seems to take charge of one particular aspect or dimension, the significance of which is partly concrete, partly abstract. Polytheism is thus more complex than Zeus appears to suggest on Olympus and his great knight Dumézil implies when he boldly separates one mode of action from another. For now, let us simply note that Dumézil's work, whose very principles proved so inspiring to others, followed on in direct line from the socioanthropology of Marcel Mauss, with its insistence on seeking categories and classifications. In those days, nothing seemed more innovative and stimulating than considering the "gods as a society," a vast "classification system": Mitra and Varuna, enclosed

---

12 *Iliad* V 330–430. In Martin Hammond's translation.

in their sovereignty, suggested a formal principle of classification; the formulas of tripartition revealed structured groups, concepts, ways of classifying the major forces that drive the world and society. Picking out categories in archaic societies and listing the forms of classification at work in mythologies and religious systems are undertakings that have continued to help us to gain a better understanding of the human spirit, considered in the context of its history and in all its variations.

All the same, by suggesting at a certain point in his inquiry that the gods, rather than being defined by the range of positions that they may occupy, can be characterized by the intentions and means of their actions, Dumézil placed the analysts of polytheisms in danger of reinforcing that most traditional of paradigms, the "individuated god," the god who can be confidently identified and recognized from a number of constant features. What we seemed to have gained by noting the entire range of positions that a deity occupied in the polytheistic system as a whole, we were in danger of losing by switching to the model of a static pantheon, inhabited by agent-gods individually classified according to a single, constant mode of action. By allowing himself to be drawn into defining a "patron-god" on the basis of his fundamental characteristics and his specific mode of action, Dumézil returned us to the starting position of classic pantheon analysis. Those laboring patiently and stubbornly over a monograph in the form of a thesis savored their triumph: their choice had been right, and as for their careers, there could continue to be no better, given the judgment of their historian peers and the confidence shown by their own "patron" in this vale of tears.

The time has now come for me to propose *experimenting* in the field of polytheisms, in particular those most familiar to me, that is to say first and foremost the gods of Greece. It is now about twenty-five years since I first tried to pinpoint the differences between divine powers who seemed to share a common field of activity—one that included equestrian skills, navigation and metallurgy—but who appeared to intervene there in quite different ways. My study took the form of a series of analyses directly inspired by the two principles established by Dumézil: (1) that in order to define a divine power, it is necessary to review the whole series of positions occupied by that deity in the polytheistic system as a whole; and (2) that one should begin by studying the habitual groupings and the religious and mythical associations between two or more divine powers, in order to explore the nature of their respective relations, first in the most explicit contexts and then, progressively, in others less obvious and less familiar. Those two principles provoked an immediate critical reaction from the historians of Greek religion who considered themselves the institutional guarantors of monographic inter-pretations.[13] My "structural" analyses were conducted within the framework of research into the forms and configurations of cunning intelligence. They focused on Athena and Poseidon, and Athena and Hephaestus, endeavoring to pick out the differential characteristics of gods who were associated together through one particular form of practical intelligence which, however, each of them oriented in rather different ways. It seemed judicious to describe these different inflections against the common background of *mêtis*, 'cunning intelligence', which had itself been represented in the form of Metis, a divine power of cosmogonic rank who, however, had at an early stage been swal-lowed by the future sovereign of Olympus.[14] I think it was useful to make a close study of the technical skills possessed in common by several gods, such as metallurgy—at which Athena, Hephaestus, and the Telchines are all adept—navigation, and "the ways of making use of the horse," a domain in which Athena and Poseidon are the foremost experts.

Without summarizing those analyses, let me indicate their limita-tions from the "experimental" point of view that I propose to defend today. In the period from 1970 to 1974, it seemed to me illuminating to proceed to analyze, on the basis of a cult common to both Poseidon and Athena—the former being known as *Hippios*, the latter as *Hippia*—the configuration of two powers associated with horses, one of them equine, the other equestrian, two powers that apparently shared the domain of horses. These two great powers confronted each other in a complementary relationship that was particularly strongly marked in Corinth: there, Poseidon presided over the violence, the impetuousness, and the disturbing and uncontrollable strength of the animal, while Athena manifested herself by acting through the horse's bit, the technical metal instrument that made it possible to gain intelligent mastery over the animal and all its natural force. The analysis of 1970–1974 concentrated on the respective modes of action of each of the two powers, focusing, in the context of "cunning intelligence," primarily on everything that underlined the *mêtis* aspect of Athena, who is sometimes known as the daughter of Metis and Zeus, but is sometimes herself identified as the highest embodiment of *mêtis* among the gods. That analysis, which was conducted by comparing a selection of stories and rituals and which discovered a number

---

13 It was in their name that F. Robert wrote a critical review of my work entitled "Artémis et Athéna" (1976).

14 Detienne and Vernant 1978:175–259.

of configurations similar to the initial "Corinthian" picture, came to suggest the idea that one could conduct a series of experiments that might immediately cast doubt on the criterion of a single, constant mode of action: simple enough experiments such as, for example, analyzing the horse with respect to both its "Athena" aspect and its "Poseidon" aspect; then setting each or both "experimentally" alongside, in the first place, the god of war, Ares—rich in horses and also in sacrificed horses—then Hera, the deity of Argos, so eager for "sovereign power" and so bellicose, if not positively warrior-like, for Zeus' wife is also overtly *hippia*. Another possible comparison might involve Poseidon: the Demeter of Arcadia, a black Demeter with a horse's head, an Erinys Demeter, and the horse Arion, born as a result of a mare-Demeter being mounted by a stallion-Poseidon. It would be a matter of seeing if any aspect of Ares, set in comparison to Athena or to Demeter confronted with Poseidon, could suddenly reveal a hitherto unsuspected dimension to horses, whether harnessed, mounted, or untamed, with or without a bit, destructive or inspired. And, conversely, this could provide a chance to detect in the resulting configuration certain dimensions of Ares, Hera, and Demeter which yet other manipulations might make it possible to confirm, correct, or reject.

By undertaking such experiments, an analyst of the Greek gods gets as close as possible to the factual data of the polytheistic field selected. What we, along with the Greeks themselves, call the domain of the *polutheos*, the plurality of divine powers, is revealed by page after page of Pausanias' *Description of Greece*, written at the time of Hadrian, and equally by every engraved stone that testifies to a city calendar or that confirms an association of deities within a single sanctuary, on a single altar, or in the organization of a particular sacrificial ritual. The grouping of gods is an essential aspect of the religious landscape of Greece, whether in major panhellenic sanctuaries or in remote country villages. Thus, in the great temple of Apollo in Delphi, Pausanias noticed an altar to Poseidon, and other documents show that two other deities also shared this space: Gaia and Hestia.[15] Moving on to Achaea, close to Patras, in the little city of Pharae, we find, in the public square, a quadrangular, bearded Hermes standing alongside the altar of Hestia, the deity of the public hearth. Furthermore, in this case, the Hermes-Hestia couple is activated by a ritual of divination. A little further on, in the same city, Pausanias came upon a field strewn with stones: thirty quadrangular, anonymous, unsculpted pillars. Now, on certain occasions, the citizens of Pharae would come to this place scattered with standing stones: "These

---

15 Pausanias 10.24.4.

[the stones] the people of Pharae adore, calling each by the name of some god."[16] Now let us proceed to Argos, this time in the company of Aeschylus. To this place the daughters of Danaus came, fleeing from their cousins, all the way from Egypt. Outside the city stood a little hill, a kind of sanctuary, filled with gods. Some were immediately recognized by the Danaids: Zeus Helios, the sun god, and Apollo. Others could be identified from particular distinguishing marks: Poseidon from his trident, Hermes from his wand. They shared altars in common.[17] How were they arranged? In groups of three, of two, of five? Such combinations could vary from place to place, as is clearly shown by the case of the "Twelve Gods": in Olympia, they are grouped into six couples; in Delos, there are four altars, each devoted to three gods. But no doubt they could equally well be disposed in two groups of six or three groups of four. Now let us consider the calendar of Erchia (an Attic deme), published in 1963.[18] Col. A. 44 and col. D. 33 show that on the same day of the month of Elaphebolion, there was a sacrifice to Semele, and one to Dionysus, involving a goat and a college of women. The two sacrifices were made on the same altar. The animal's skin went to the priestess and the meat was divided up, *ou phora*, to be consumed on the spot. In Gamelion D. 30 (and B. 37 and G. 40), three other gods were associated: there was a sacrifice to Poseidon on the same day and in the same place as a sacrifice offered to Zeus *Teleios* and to Hera. The place where this happened was the sanctuary of Hera, in Erchia. For this sacrifice, Hera was in the position of host. And Poseidon was directly associated with the couple that protected marriage. But how and why? Meanwhile, on the altar to Amphiarus, twelve stadia distant from Oropos, eighteen deities stood on the altar table, which was divided into five sections. And in Claros, in Asia Minor, in the great oracular sanctuary of Apollo, the principal altar was shared by Dionysus and Apollo.

Polytheism in Greece finds expression on the ground, on altars, in temples, in sacrificial rules, and in figurative representations. The evidence that Greek culture provides for historians of religion takes the form of established groupings, organized relations between two or several powers, explicit relations of opposition or complementarity between deities. "Structures" are immediately manifest. At both the local and the Panhellenic levels, Greek pantheons present a rich variety of groups of gods, manifestations of hierarchies, symmetrical configurations of antagonisms or affinities. In choosing to

16 Pausanias 7.22.4. Translation of W. H. S. Jones.
17 Aeschylus *Suppliant Maidens* 189–222.
18 See Sokolowski 1969, no. 18, 36–44.

work on groupings and configurations of divine powers, an analyst of Greek polytheisms manifests a resolute pragmatism, if not "positivism." As historians with a monographic approach lazily continue to classify the "elementary structures" of the pantheon under the rubric of "associations" between one god and another, as the *Altertumswissenschaft* has always done,[19] the analyst of polytheisms will draw their attention to the countless recurrences of associations and groupings of deities throughout antiquity, from Homer down to Porphyry, ranging from Zeus' remarks about the Olympians' respective "domains of authority" all the way down to the religious rules, dedications, and calendars of the Greek cities of the Hellenistic period. For at least ten centuries the Greeks had the same gods, used the same sanctuaries, and followed the same ritual practices, although that by no means ruled out local changes and contextual variations. The long survival of Greek polytheism provides an analyst with a field of experimentation in which, it would seem, full use has not yet been made of all the epigraphical discoveries and works of erudition that continue to enrich and, in many cases, renew our knowledge of pantheons and religious practices.

Ever since historians began to write the history of religious thought and the history of the gods of Greece, the question of origins, if not that of etymology, has fascinated them as much as, if not more than, the question of what became of those gods — the vicissitudes that a deity might encounter as it passed from one sanctuary to another, or as it moved on from a particular configuration in one particular spot to become an isolated and dominant figure, at the invitation of a particular city at a particular moment in its history.[20] According to F. Robert and others, historical evolution is the making of the gods, and also, no doubt, of everything else. I have no definitive reason to reject any inquiry that claims to find in history and its events the key to a particular grouping of gods or to a particular assembly of powers round some altar or in some sanctuary. But perhaps one could fairly object to a historian seeking for origins that he or she is obliged to fix arbitrarily on the initial content of a god's "personality" before it becomes enriched—or impoverished (why not?)—by the fortuitous march of history and all its accidents. It is true that no analyst of polytheism can interpret or recognize a configuration or even a simple pair of powers without already having some idea of the silhouette or manner of Athena, Poseidon, or Apollo, as the case

---

19 In one of its major—it must be said—indispensable productions, *Paulys Realencyclopädie der classischen Altertumswissenschaft.*
20 This is the view of F. Robert 1976.

may be. Nevertheless, even if it is not considered prejudicial to believe that Athena is, for example, a "parcel of fetishes"[21] (snake, *palladion*, and so on), more or less securely tied together, or that Apollo is certainly a Hittite god, or rather a brutal and violent Asiatic, the kind of experimental analyst that I have in mind will feel more free to study how groupings are organized and, above all, whether they are variable and diversified, to undertake in-depth analyses of the coherence of certain configurations, and to see how the most deeply contrasted gods react in relation to one another.

In the field of Greek polytheisms, the surest way for an experimental approach to proceed is by conducting litmus tests using concrete objects, rather than by engineering direct confrontations between integral powers whose individuated characteristics, however implicit, disrupt the effects of the experimental procedure.[22] The surest, if not the most direct way to analyze whole complexes of relations between deities and to avoid being led astray by the immediate forms of gods so prone, ever since the days of their original native devotees, to become individuals, is to approach them by way of concrete details and segments of situations: through objects, gestures, and situations. In our study of the links between the gods with *mêtis*, we mentioned some of those objects: the bit, the horse, the ship, the rudder; and some of those concrete gestures or actions: guiding, traveling, crossing, defining limits; as well as certain situations whose provisional institutional context would be war, marriage, agriculture, death, or birth, all of which would produce a profusion of concrete and, in principle, limitless gestures and objects. It is not hard to draw up a list of them. Here is a sample, in alphabetical order: bow, dolphin, nightingale, seal, spear, spindle, winnowing basket, and so on. Even the so-called scholars and historians of religions, curious about the "attributes" of certain gods, have frequently (and most usefully) studied what they call their "symbolisms," and have in this way produced fragmentary encyclopedias and conglomerations of religious representations. But it was the ethnologists, first and foremost Lévi-Strauss, who revealed the wealth of concrete objects, gestures, and situations that can be used to further our understanding of the mythical tales and adventures of supernatural characters.[23] They have shown us that any object, with—in principle—an infinite number of features, can be associated with other objects in limitless series of associations. This is where a knowledge of the ethnographic context comes in, for it is this that helps an

---

21 F. Robert 1976:152.
22 The image of a litmus test is suggested by Dumézil 1954:74.
23 This is seen in Lévi-Strauss throughout his works from "La geste d'Asdiwal" (1958) onward, but in particularly illuminating fashion in his more recent work: *Histoire de Lynx* (1995).

analyst of polytheist complexes to learn everything possible about the fauna, the flora, and the customary practices of games, hunting, and warfare; about, in fact, all the material and concrete aspects of a particular culture. Whether they are reading mythical tales or studying configurations of the gods, Greek scholars, for instance, need to be familiar with not only rituals, calendars, and religious rules but also the native treatises on plants, animals, stones, minerals, and techniques—everything that will enable them to "plug into the cultural network," in much the same way as ethnologists in their villages or engrossed in an ethnic group about which the Observers of Mankind have had the patience to write an encyclopedia.[24]

Experimental procedures are familiar to comparatists who, like Lévi-Strauss, undertake to compare two different systems, taking some well-defined object, easily isolated, the different states of which, revealed by observation, can be analyzed by studying just a few variables, sometimes reducing their number, sometimes concentrating on those of the same type. It is true that Dumézil, for his part, on more than one occasion preferred to give priority to points of similarity. But frequently also, in the course of studying the warrior function (the Third Hero killing a triple adversary), he strove to make out how each of the societies being compared imagined the destiny of the "Third Hero" once the murder had been committed, and he thereby showed that there were at least four ways of avoiding the consequences of a necessary killing.[25] Dumézil had the idea of paying attention to internal interactions and significant details in order to test the impact of the tripartite structure on a whole series of "notions or categories both concrete and abstract" which at first sight seem important in all societies or, more particularly, in the Indo-European ones that constituted his own field of research.[26] Objects, gestures, and segments of situations constitute "litmus tests," that is to say things that provoke a reaction when in contact with a power, an object, or a gesture that then reveals some hitherto unnoticed aspect, a hidden property, or an unexpected angle. The most simple principle of such experimentation is to find out "what happens." For instance, Dumézil showed us what happens when what is involved is a horse[27]—by no means a random choice in a "civilization" in which the warrior function, with its horse-drawn chariots, was responsible for such overwhelming conquests.

---

24 This was the method that I adopted in *The Gardens of Adonis* (1994a), returning to consider the subject more attentively in the afterword, "Revisiting the Gardens of Adonis" (133–144).
25 See Dumézil (1967).
26 This aspect has been emphasized by a Latin interpreter of Dumézil, J. Scheid 1983:343–354.
27 See Dumézil 1954:73–91; 1966:276–78.

When placed in contact with a qualified representative of each of the three functions, the horse revealed three different aspects of its animal nature and at the same time drew attention to a number of features of the tripartition. When attached to the *quadriga* of a sovereign god, the horse manifests the power of the triumphant victor, advancing under the sign of Jupiter, whose priest was forbidden ever to mount this noble animal, let alone to offer it up as a sacrifice. When offered as a sacrifice to the god of war—to Mars—the same animal exalts the warrior virtues and the qualities of death; in contact with the third function, the horse is simply a member of the horse family and becomes a beast of burden on a par with a mule or a donkey. Had there been five functions in the Indo-European world, the horse would have had an extra two qualities. Similarly, the object constituted by the horse's bit, which seems to be absent from the Indo-European domain, may serve as a litmus test in a configuration comprising, in different forms of association, various Greek deities such as Athena, Poseidon, the Telchines, Hephaestus, and others.

It is by paying attention to whatever is most concrete that the microanalyst finds the means of experimentally probing the configurations of divine powers, and it is these that constitute the primary data and elementary forms available to an observer of polytheisms in Greece. Consider, for example, a god such as Apollo, well known ever since the *Iliad* to be involved in a number of important configurations.[28] Through his epithets, his cults, and his rituals, he presents an attentive observer with a number of very concrete modes of behavior to which both the Homeric epic and the sixth-century BCE *Hymn* dedicated to him testify directly. Throughout Greece and over many centuries, Apollo was known as *Aguieus*: the god of paths, roads, and networks of ways. He opened up routes and marked out paths with stones, stones that were carried by his sixth-century BCE priests in a seventeen-kilometer-long procession from the gates of his Milesian sanctuary to the gates of the sanctuary of Apollo in Didyma. Stones were positioned along routes for him, and carried in procession for him, and meanwhile Apollo was himself given a figurative cult presence as a pillar. The *Homeric Hymn to Apollo* tells us at length of how the god born on Delos would lay out sites, set his foot down firmly there, backtrack, and carve out territories, always organizing space thanks to his mastery of the network of paths that traversed it. There is an extensive concrete vocabulary for the interpreter to study: Apollo sets his foot down, clears the land, places stones, founds territories. For this god starts by clearing a way through the thickets, orients his journey through the "primitive forest" (*hulê*, which later came to mean

---

28 For the necessary references and comments, see Detienne 1998a.

'matter'). Better still, he builds his own roads and, once arrived in Delphi, he sets about laying down stone foundations, raising walls, and sinking the threshold slab into position. He is an architect and a founder, in the fullest sense of the term. Along the paths of Apollo, which intersect with those of Hermes and the crossroads of Hecate, and pass through the sanctuaries of Poseidon, stones are carried, moved from one place to another, to be set down and fixed in particular places. And there are thresholds to be laid down, crossed, and defended; doors to be made and to be protected; precincts to be plotted out; boundaries to be established, walked around, and prohibited to others.

What does a microanalyst do when faced with these stones and doors? Certainly not waste time wondering whether they constitute "proof" of a transition from aniconic to anthropomorphic figurative representation. The Apollo Belvedere coexists, quite indifferently, with an Apollo-pillar or an Apollo in the form of a conical stone, which is how the ordinary everyday *aguieus* is represented. The microanalyst knows from a whole series of epithets and a study of how things are organized that the god Hermes, Apollo's little brother, shares with the god of Delos, Delphi, and Megara a whole set of qualities relating to doors and paths, thresholds and stones, precincts and altars; not to mention music, musical instruments, and speech and its effects. That is the field of experimentation and manipulations that await the analyst.

By this stage in the inquiry, an analyst who has not thought it necessary to go armed from the start with an identity card for Apollo, is nevertheless in possession of a number of concrete indications relating to this god and, thanks to these, can glimpse certain orientations within a domain that is recognizably more or less Apollonian, for that has already been realized as a "domain" that overlaps with the fields of activity of several other powers, some of which are associated together regularly, others only occasionally. The time has come for the second stage in the analyst's investigation, that of choosing one particular configuration within the Apollonian field and seeking out the reason for the grouping or the significance of the interconnections that the analyst will try to detect, testing them out against all that is known of polytheisms and the society which, as evidence shows, uses them. The configuration in the sanctuary of Delphi, for example, gathers around Apollo, Poseidon, and Hestia, and also Gaia, along with Themis; and to these powers we should add Dionysus, who was certainly not the last to arrive in this select circle assembled around the Pythian oracle. As a rule, a microanalyst, confronted with a grouping of gods, prefers a couple or a triad rather than a gathering as complex as that surrounding Apollo in Delphi. With a pair such as Hestia-Hermes or Apollo-Hermes, the analysis may adopt one of two methods. The first is to undertake an internal exploration of what each of the two powers stands for, testing them out in the context of stories, cults, rituals, and institutions, some of which at the same time encourage the joint or opposed actions of the two deities, who thus seem to express the structure of a pantheon. The other method, which seems to me to be complementary to the first, is to study the reactions of the Hestia-Hermes or Apollo-Hermes pair by placing them in contact with all the other groupings available, frequently making the most of the explicit relations between them, and starting with those that are closest to the original pair, such as Hestia-Apollo-Poseidon, Hermes-Aphrodite-Hestia, Poseidon-Gaia-Apollo-Themis. Either way, the approach remains experimental and aims to uncover sets of underlying relations.

The configuration of Apollo in Delphi emerges from the founding footsteps of a god who, with care, can be apprehended through the objects, gestures, and concrete situations that come to characterize him as he makes his way from Delos to Delphi. The best way to track down Gaia, Poseidon, and Hestia is to follow Apollo's journey step by step, as it is recounted in the *Homeric Hymn* devoted to him. The verb *ktizein* links the gesture of clearing the way, cutting a path through a primitive forest, with the act of establishing something in an enduring fashion, or of founding. Parallel to this, the action signified by *bainein* and its compounds indicates moving from one place to another, treading firmly with "a sure foot." Apollo's tread causes things to tremble. His foot is that of a soccer kicker; it is shattering and always makes its mark. Solidly positioned, the god protects towns and territories, his legs firmly straddled "on either side." His stability is comparable to that of a well-constructed road linking one point to another, a road with both a beginning and an end, an *arkhê* and a *telos*. In all his Apollonian stability, the god encounters the only deity to be found on the journey to Delphi. This is not Gaia, but Poseidon: the Poseidon of Onchestos who, in his sacred wood, reigns over the newly tamed horse and the harnessed chariot. Poseidon is *already there*. In Delphi he catches up with Apollo and offers him "a pure base" (*dapeda*), flattened ground upon which his nephew, a founder through and through, sets the *themeilia*, the threshold stone, the load-bearing walls, everything that needs a base and setting that is sure (*asphaleios*), a quality in which Poseidon is well tried, particularly on sites where he is presented as Apollo's accomplice and cofounder, where Apollo assumes the role of *arkhêgetês*, leaving to his uncle the responsibilities of *themelioukhos*, the one who solidly holds the foundations fast.

The presence of the couple formed by Apollo and Poseidon in the temple of Delphi, along with the marginal position of a small sanctuary consecrated to Gaia, suggest that we should not subscribe to the belief of Delphian archaeologists for whom an Earth who is manifestly oracular is altogether in harmony with this natural site that has a mantic vocation and that boasts, along with its spring and its trees, a cleft in the rock and a laurel bush. As is well known, after one hundred years of excavating Delphi with a fine-tooth comb, nothing at all has been found to indicate the presence of a Gê with a prophetic activity. Here in Delphi, Gaia is mute, just as she is at Olympia, representing a stage in her existence that came before she ever manifested any oracular powers by dispensing advice to the future gods. As a marginal figure associated with the temple of Apollo and situated out there on the Delphic horizon, Earth without a doubt represents a base forever secure, the very base implied by the Poseidon of "pure foundations." This is not the Gaia whom some prefer to see as a *paredros* (a term meaning an assessor of other deities, frequently used in the inflexible language of the history of religions). Rather, this is the Earth known as the Well-Founded One (*Euthemethlos*), because she is self-founded, in herself. Just beneath the surface it becomes possible to make out the hierarchy by which Delphi is inhabited: the Self-founded Earth, Poseidon the Establisher of Bases, and Apollo the Builder-Founder.

Hestia, who is enthroned at the heart of Apollo's dwelling, is also related to Earth, through Rheia, her grandmother. Both for the Pythia and for the sacrificers who came to consult her, Hestia's strength of endurance and her quality of stability are represented by the hearth, the altar-hearth of the house. This is the Hestia who, for all Greek cities, became the "pure and eternal" Fire, the Common Hearth, but who was also a power favoring new cities, with their own altars and their own Prytaneis. She is also Hestia *Dômatitês*, active in the construction of homes, and courted in her own by both Apollo and Poseidon, both of whom are known as *dômatitis* and are characterized by their attraction to Hestia's fine stability, her "unshakable basis," which uncle and nephew alike consider so very desirable. Where oracular speech was concerned, however, Apollo expected nothing from Hestia, and she was left as mute as Poseidon.

Meanwhile, the young god's nurse, Themis, far from presiding over "the oracles of Earth," is instituted as the deity who, intimately connected with Apollo, leads one toward the *themistes*, the "founding words," or *thesmoi*, the "decrees" issued by the Lord of Delphi when he speaks and *themisteuei*. Themis mediates between Gaia and Apollo, and is seated close to the oracular tripod, as a Pythia who can imbue prophetic speech with its most important meanings. As the mother of both the *Moirai* (the two Shares, led by the Apollo *Moiragetês*) and also the *Horai* (the Seasons, who regulate the social order), Themis reveals herself to be an expert at telling of both the present and the future in her decrees, imbuing oracular speech with its foundational power from her position in the divinatory sanctuary that was the very first to be established, before any other foundation, by Apollo, her nursling.

Another way to penetrate this complex would be by way of *bainein*, which leads to an Apollo "from the seashore," a "maritime" god known now as *Embasios*, now as *Ekbasios*, a god who embarks and disembarks, and who thus crosses the paths of Poseidon, Athena, and Hera. This is an Apollo who, through the Argonauts' expedition, was related to the consultation of the oracle, to the authorization of departures and returns, and to modalities of intervention very close to those revealed by the building of ships, navigation, and the perils of the sea, considered from the point of view of other more or less "maritime" powers.

By proceeding in this fashion, an analyst of the configurations of polytheism remains free to take apart and reassemble what Clifford Geertz would call "the partial logics of thought." Instead of choosing, right from the start and perhaps unconsciously, between two robotic portraits of a god such as Apollo—on the one hand, that of a god of moral superiority (W. F. Otto), on the other, that of a god of terrible violence (J. Defradas)—the microanalyst can break things up, focus on details. The more he restricts the field of comparison—for instance, to the foot and the threshold, in the case of Hermes and Apollo—the more possible differences and distinctions he will discover between those two powers and likewise between others incorporated into that particular comparison. It cannot fail to be interesting to see how Poseidon, Hestia, and Heracles react to a threshold, or to the movement of a foot, or to a stone, whether this be carried or fixed upright in the ground.

All of these are ways of penetrating the tiny systems of thought that are embedded in gatherings and groupings of gods, of seeing how, as G. Lenclud suggests, the adoption of one particular element of thought or one particular rule of action prompts a culture to make a choice, and of detecting what constraints are at work in the configuration selected, given its cultural context. Perhaps "manipulation" would be a better word to use than "experimentation." For experimentation necessitates coming back repeatedly to the phenomena observed and possibly altering the conditions under which the experiment is carried out. Manipulation, on the other hand, may cover what I mean when I speak of bringing into contact and prompting reactions between phenomena and configurations that are never repeated in precisely the same form in the course of history; phenomena and configurations which, however, in a single culture probed deeply throughout its duration, may recur formally in contexts sufficiently varied to reveal the transformations that may be undergone by some of the elements composing them.

Let me repeat my position: the experimental approach that I am proposing in no way sets out to dismiss the characteristics that make up the style of the polytheism of the Greeks: namely the fact that the forms (*skhê-mata*) of the Olympians were already clearly indicated at the dawn of Homeric culture; that, at the hands of painters and sculptors, the figures of the gods early on and everywhere acquired individual characteristics; that poets and craftsmen working with words constantly surrounded the great gods with strictly personalized stories and eulogies; and that, depending on the place and the time, the settings of polytheism were modified and redrawn for particular and deliberate purposes. The freedom with which certain political assemblies reorganized the calendar of festivals and the hierarchy of sacrifices constitutes an important indication of the nature of polytheistic practice in Greece. But as they acted thus, the Greek cities were not reorganizing the gods in a haphazard or arbitrary fashion; rather, they were experimenting, on a day-to-day basis, with certain combinations made possible by the system.

By drawing attention to all that is not stated explicitly about the gods and their powers, I should like to encourage analysts of polytheistic complexes to investigate the way in which the divine powers are linked in dozens of aspects with the objects and phenomena of social life and the natural world. To be sure, it is possible to relate the gods to one another explicitly in configurations presented in stories that are either mythological or "theological," in the Greek sense. But firstly they are bound together in a series of micronetworks which reveal them as interacting in a complex fashion throughout the entire cultural field. Only by dint of repeated manipulations will we gradually come to glimpse the richness of the polytheistic fabric in societies where, for one thing, every god is *plural*.

2

This Is Where I Intend to Build a Glorious Temple[*]

BEFORE MAKING ONE OF THE MOST decisive pronouncements of his career, the young Apollo had experienced what it was to wander, for even before his birth, his doubly pregnant mother was forced to undertake a long march.[1] The story of this great god starts from humble beginnings. Apollo was born furtively, far from the fine dwellings of Olympus. He first saw the light of day in a remote corner of the Aegean Sea. His first steps were taken among people doomed to live "witless and helpless," that is to say, mortals (*Homeric Hymn to Apollo* 191–192).

Apollo belonged to the race of Zeus. He knew it and let others know it. But in the first place, he was the son of Leto, Leto the fugitive, a pregnant mistress cast out to roam the highways and byways. Apollo's mother was also of high lineage: she was the daughter of Phoebe, and the granddaughter of Sky and Earth, chosen by Zeus to give birth to the fairest and most powerful of his sons. For the time being, however, Leto was hounded by the jealousy of Hera (89–114), Zeus' legitimate wife, and his third, following Metis and Themis. Leto travelled at night, like a she-wolf (some said she even took this form[2]), beseeching in turn the plains, the mountains, and the islands to give her asylum, a home for her son, and to allow her to found a rich sanctuary (30–50). But all of them "greatly trembled and feared" (47). None had the

---

[*] Originally published in *Arion* 4.3 (Winter 1997) 1–27.

[1] The English translation used for the text is that by Hugh G. Evelyn-White in the Loeb Classical Library; verse numbers henceforth cited parenthetically in text. On the *Homeric Hymn to Apollo*, an extremely useful work is Miller 1986. The philology on the text comes from Allen, Halliday, and Sikes 1936, and also from Humbert 1959.

[2] According to Aristotle *History of Animals* VI 35, 580a16–20, Leto became a she-wolf in order to avoid being seen by Hera; it took her twelve days to travel from the land of the Hyperboreans to Delos. This was why there were only twelve days in the year when she-wolves produced their young. Cf. Aelian *De natura animalium* X 26.

courage to take her in; the richest lands and the best-established sires were the first to decline the honor of welcoming the future Apollo. Only one island, the smallest and poorest of all, heeded Leto's prayer and declared itself ready to become the land of Apollo (51–88).

That island was Delos, a rock lost amid the waves, a refuge for seals and octopuses. According to Callimachus, it was a kind of floating island,[3] but one that took root once it became the home and seat of the new god. Before committing itself, Delos hesitated for a moment: what if Apollo scorned it, dispatched it with a great kick to the bottom of the sea? Leto reassured the island and swore a great oath by the gods: this was where Apollo would make his home forever (66–73).[4]

There were nine days and nine nights of pain, amid a great gathering of goddesses, including some of the most noble; then Eilithyia, long detained by Hera, at last arrived, and the child burst forth into the light (89–126). Themis hastened to present the newborn infant with nectar and ambrosia (124–125). Already Leto's son was feeling constrained in his swaddling bands, and now he asked for his lyre and his bow: "'The lyre and the curved bow shall ever be dear to me, and I will declare to men the unfailing will of Zeus'" (131–132). Even as he let fly his first words, Apollo "began to walk (*epibasken*) upon the wide-pathed earth" (133). Then followed another long march that was eventually to lead the god to the chosen site where he would build "a glorious temple" (247–248). The Apollonian way of "creating a territory" was to be revealed by the actions and adventures that took place in the course of the journey from Delos to Delphi.[5]

Right from the start of the *Hymn* that associates the glory of Delos and the magnificence of the sanctuary in Delphi, Apollo cuts an impressive figure as a god on the move. His step rings out in the first two lines: "I will remember and not be unmindful of Apollo who shoots afar, for whom the gods tremble in the

---

3 Callimachus *Hymn to Delos* 273: *plagktê*. Cf. Detienne and Vernant 1978:253n74.
4 Delos refers to *atasthalos* nature of Apollo: his excessively "proud," "violent," if not brutal character. I shall return to this point.
5 We shall be following Apollo's itinerary from Delos to Delphi for the simple reason that his founding of the oracle concludes the journey of the god who, while still in Delos, proclaimed his power over the lyre, the bow, and prophecy. This "unitary" reading makes it possible to sidestep the stormy debates between philologists over the differences between the "Delian" part of the *Hymn* and the "Pythian" part. Those debates are elegantly summarized in Clay 1989:18–19. Her commentary on the *Hymn to Apollo* (17–94) tackles the question of "panhellenism" in the organization of the pantheon in a very helpful manner.

house of Zeus as they hear him approach (*ionta*)" (1–2).[6] In the version of the story presented in the *Homeric Hymn*, Apollo the Archer impetuously claims precedence over Apollo the Lyre Player. The first sight of him as he arrives at Olympus is of a god brandishing (*titainei*) a curved bow (4).[7] This Apollo is characterized by strength, power, and even brutality. The assembled gods scatter before him, and his mother hastens to calm him down with soothing words, leading him to his seat and urging him toward his father (6–9). A little further on in the *Hymn*, Apollo's second manifestation contrasts sharply with the first. The adolescent Apollo, with shoulder-length locks,[8] takes his first steps on the island of Delos, which is "laden with gold" in its joy at having been chosen as the home of the son of Zeus and Leto. The gaze of Phoebus, still called the Archer, now takes in Delos in all its festivity (147–176) and is delighted at the sight of the Ionians gathered there. The island is giddy with singing, dancing, and games: such is the grace of the Ionians' performance that they could be mistaken for immortals who never age (150–151). Imperceptibly, amid this mixture of a vision and a manifestation, the gap between mortals and immortals shrinks away. To Apollo's eyes, the festive crowd singing the god's praises seems like a gathering of the gods on Olympus, engaged in the Muses' songs and dances.[9] The god of the bow suddenly becomes Apollo the Lyre Player, as he heads for rocky Pytho, carried away by the music. As "swift as thought" (182–206), Apollo now speeds from earth to Olympus, to the house of his father, where he joins the other gods gathered there. This time, there is no fear or consternation: "The undying gods think only of the lyre and song" (188). To the sound of the lyre, the striding Apollo becomes a dancer "with a high, prancing step" (201). The Muses, the daughters of Memory, raise their lovely voices to hymn the joys of the Olympian gods and remind their listeners of the fate of those doomed to die (187–193). Up there on Olympus, fleeting resemblances melt away as snow in the sunshine: among themselves the gods are all too aware of the trials that beset those half-alive beings who are so inadequate that they can devise neither a remedy for death nor a way

---

6 On "unmindful," see Simondon 1982:55–59.

7 *Titainein* 'to draw, bend' (the bow). The verb also evokes the behavior of a Titan, which is similar to that of a god who is *atasthalos* and boundlessly presumptuous.

8 *Akersokomês*: *Hymn to Apollo* 134. Apollo, the *kouros*, the ephebe, the god who presides over the development of the young Telemachus (*Odyssey* xix 86). In Actium, the regulations for the festival of Apollo prescribed "allowing one's hair to grow," wearing it long: Sokolowski 1962, no. 45, l. 41–43. At the end of the *Hymn to Apollo* 449–450, Apollo reappears to his ministers as a robust, strong man in his first youth.

9 Cf. Frontisi-Ducroux 1986:62–74.

of avoiding old age. There would come a time when a "distant" Apollo would take care to draw attention to the abyss separating the race of men from the Olympian gods. But for the time being this was simply an interlude under the signs of the bow and the lyre, the two instruments of power that the son of Leto claimed as his own.

The god then returned to Delos, from which he set out to accomplish a project that he was soon to announce explicitly, a project that involved building, establishing, and founding. The time had come to seek the right spot (215). A first quick look round (19–24):[10] Delos afforded a panoramic view.[11] At a glance Apollo could see all the provinces of his empire, Lycia, "lovely Maeonia and Miletus, charming city by the sea,"[12] with "a bird's-eye view"[13] that ranged from the topmost peaks, taking in the mountain ranges, down to the valleys and the rivers flowing to the sea. Then he strode off, at a steady pace, exploring regions as yet unknown, crossing plains, hugging the coast, climbing hills: place names crowd one upon another in this wild landscape with overlapping paths.[14]

On the way to Crisa, three sites marked out the route of the god known throughout the Greek world as the god of paths, *aguieus*.[15] Leaving his birthplace, Apollo made his way over an as yet untouched space, crossing vast expanses, discovering blank, empty landscapes. First he came to Euboea, the Lelantine plain, a dreary wasteland: whoever would want to build a temple here (219–221)? Apollo rejected it and pressed on in the direction of Teumessus, making for Mycalessus. In fact, the seemingly featureless Euboean landscape did contain a site upon which an important Apollonian sanctuary had stood ever since the eighth century—over a century before the earliest possible date for this *Hymn*. This was the *Daphnêphorion*, the "temple of laurel," discovered in Eretria by Swiss archaeologists.[16] As he marched on to the place where he would eventually carry out his intention of "building a glorious temple," there

---

10 At the very beginning, before the quest of 215. Cf. Roux 1964.

11 Again, *Hymn to Apollo*; there are no toponyms, only geographical references to high peaks, mountain ranges, valleys, rivers, the sea, beaches, and headlands.

12 The names are mentioned in lines 179–180. Cf. Miller 1986:66.

13 Roux 1964:6. Falcons and merlins are "Apollonian" birds.

14 One itinerary leads from Olympus, by sea, passing by way of Chalcis to Telphusion; the other leads from the south by sea around the Peloponnese and ends up at the altar of Apollo *Delphinios*, at Crisa. Cf. Defradas 1972:70–71; Miller 1986:56–70.

15 The data is collected by Cook 1925:160–166. More recently, see Balestrazzi 1980–81:93–108, whose conclusions I am unable to accept.

16 Bérard 1971; Altherr-Charon and Bérard 1980.

were no paths for Apollo to follow. The Lelantine plain was as empty of traces of human occupation as was the site of Thebes, the second vista to meet the eyes of Leto's son.[17]

Here, a great forest covered the site of what would one day be Thebes of the Seven Gates, "for as yet no man lived in holy Thebes, nor were there tracks or ways about Thebes' wheat-bearing plain: nothing but dense woods (*hulê*)" (225–228).[18] Apollo was the first to open up a path through this virgin forest, for these were primeval woods in which no human being had ever set foot, a wild forest nothing like the space of a "sacred wood" (*alsos*), a clump of trees or a grove[19] carved out and arranged in the manner of just such a sanctuary as Apollo, at various stages on his journey, declared he would himself be "constructing" (*teukhein*).[20] The second blank space encountered by Apollo was thus that of Thebes before Thebes existed, where there was as yet no sign of the great gods who were one day to live there: no sign of Cadmus' grandson, Dionysus, or of the Apollo *Ismenios* who was to produce oracular signals of fire.[21]

At the time when Apollo was making his way from Euboea toward Onchestus, Thebes was still buried under a thick forest, buried there so deeply that, for the Greek memory, the very idea of the foundation of a city was always to be evoked by the name of Thebes, the Thebes of the twin brothers, Amphion and Zethus, who built its ramparts.[22] For the Town of the Seven Gates was, after all, the city where—according to Homer's epic, echoing even more ancient Theban tales[23]—the autochthonous Spartoi, strange seedlings born from the earth, had mingled with the town's true founders.

---

17 The significance of the silence reigning over the *Daphnêphorion* was first addressed in a note by Bruneau 1976.

18 Neither *atarpitoi*, nor *keleuthoi*. *Hulê* is twice repeated.

19 A meaning suggested by Robert and Robert 1981:467, in connection with Apollo *Alsenos*. On the "sacred wood" as a type of urban or extra-urban sanctuary, cf. Jacob 1993.

20 The Lelantine plain is, precisely, a place where Apollo explicitly states that he would not like to "construct" (*teukhein*) either a sanctuary (*neôs*) or "a sacred wood full of trees": *Hymn to Apollo* 221. At the end of the *Odyssey*, at xx 275–278, there is a mention of a sanctuary of Apollo to which people of Ithaca take a sacrificial offering, a sanctuary in the shape of an *alsos*.

21 Historians and philologists have drawn a variety of conclusions from this silence: Defradas 1972:58–62.

22 Vian 1963.

23 *Odyssey* iii 262–265: Amphion and Zethus were the first to found (*ektisan*) the "base" (*hedos*) of Thebes and build the ramparts (*purgôsan*), ramparts without which Thebes would have been uninhabitable and which, furthermore, were constructed "with the lyre" according to [Hesiod] fr. 182 MW; [Apollodorus] *Library* 3.42–44.

Already Onchestus could be glimpsed (230–238), another site made famous by the *Iliad* and the list of emblazoned shields.[24] Poseidon's sacred wood of Onchestus rose above the southern bank of Lake Copais.[25] Unlike the two previous sites, this third one was beautifully laid out. It was a "sacred wood," manifestly the domain of the god of chariots and horses.[26] This was where Poseidon had set up headquarters to test how "newly broken colts" would react when, upon entering the wood, their drivers leaped down from the chariot, leaving the horses on their own to cope with the terror of the place and the chassis rattling behind them. For each of these Poseidonian animals, never harnessed to a noisy chariot before, this was a moment of truth. Left to its own devices, the horse would either pass calmly through Poseidon's domain or else, disoriented by the absence of the driver and by the din made by the vehicle, the colt would be seized with panic and would smash the chariot against the trees. It would thus appear that, at the point when Apollo arrived at Onchestus on his way from Euboea, Poseidon was already ensconced there, busy exercizing a power that related to mankind and the human ability "to control a horse-drawn chariot." In the shadow of the Lord of Onchestus, whose path was again to cross Apollo's on more than one occasion, it is perhaps possible to detect the horse breeders of the land of Boeotia, a society evoked here as discreetly as were the Ionians dancing in their festive garments in the paved courts of Delos. On this long walk of Apollo's, Poseidon was the only god, the sole Olympian that he was to encounter: his own uncle, with whom he would be sharing a number of fine, major foundations after first living alongside him at Delphi. As *Gaiêokhos*, "the Lord who holds and possesses the earth," Poseidon seems to have been marked out for the role of a god of foundations, the one who is *already there* when any plan to build and lay foundations is first devised.

24 *Iliad* II 506 (an *alsos*).
25 Hermes follows along the edge of the "sacred wood" of Onchestus on his nocturnal foray to steal Apollo's cattle: *Hymn to Hermes* 186–187. Then he begins to cross through it, meeting only one individual, an "old man with the face of a brute." Hermes advises him to have seen nothing. Later, he gives Apollo confusing information. Perhaps the picture of the master of the place, Poseidon *Gaiêokhos*, disguised as an old man of the woods, is intended to be ironical.
26 I am following the intelligent interpretation of Roux 1964. Cf. Detienne and Vernant 1978:187–189. Roesch 1977 has sketched in the fortunes, between 338 and 172, of this ancient, nonurban sanctuary that became the administrative capital of Boeotia, a capital without a city. On the site of Onchestus and its cults, cf. Schachter 1986.

Pushing on "further still" (239), leaving the wood of Onchestus behind, Apollo then came to the stream of Cephissus and the fields of Haliartus and was soon treading the turf of Telphusa (244). It was a peaceful, delightful place and Apollo decided to stop there. He spoke of the site, addressing the spirit of the place and announcing: "This is where I intend to build a glorious temple" (247–248). No sooner said than done; Phoebus began to lay out the foundations of the temple (*diethêke themeilia*) (254). They were to be vast and very long. But Telphusa's voice interrupted this operation. It informed him of the hidden drawbacks to the site: the constant trampling of horses, the din of chariots and the busy crowd around them. Telphusa was twice as noisy as any Onchestus, the voice warned. In reality, as we discover—although Apollo at this point had no inkling of it—Telphusa wanted to keep all the glory of the site for herself, so she filled the ears of the builder-god with praises of another place, nearby, at the foot of the gorges of Parnassus: Crisa (255–276).[27]

Again Apollo moved on, travelling "yet further" (277). His first step brought him to the land of the Phlegyae, the first human settlement he had come across in the entire journey (278). The Phlegyae, "burning" with pride and presumption, were the very incarnation of the *hubris* that appeared to be the rule for mortals, as Apollo was to remark at the end of this *Hymn* (541). In them, *hubris* was so great that it was one day to cause every last one of them to perish in a mad attempt to loot the sanctuary of Apollo.[28] With one last stride, Apollo reached the foot of snowy Parnassus (281–282). The site seemed perfect, midway between the sea and the mountains, on a foothill facing south, with a deep valley below and steep rocks rising behind it.

"This is where I intend to build a glorious temple."[29] The builder-god repeated the same words as before, but now they were intended for no recipient, as if this place were totally empty and belonged to nobody. Again foundations were laid down and construction began (294–295). Two architect brothers emerged from the shadows, Agamedes and Trophonius, and built

---

27 Cf. Miller 1986:76–80. Telphusa occupies a central position in stories about the Erinys and Poseidon. It was there that the horse Arion was born from the love-making between them, and also there that the Erinys gave birth to the snake that Cadmus would slay before founding Thebes on top of the seeds of war (cf. Defradas 1972:68). Ares and Demeter are also connected with this "Telphusian" place. Cf. Breglia Pulci Doria 1986.

28 Pherecydes FGH 3 F41e. Cf. Vian 1963:125.

29 Following the announcement made by the pregnant Leto, this same formulation of words recurs several times in the course of Apollo's career: *Hymn to Apollo* 287 (*phroneô teuksein*). (Translation adapted.)

"a footing of stone" (296).[30] The building site hummed with activity, with a countless swarm of men working for Apollo as stonemasons (298).[31] The sanctuary of Delphi, founded at Apollo's journey's end, welcomed its founder and sanctioned the oracular powers that he would exercise: "In my oracles, I shall also reveal the infallible designs of Zeus" (292–293). The establishment of Apollonian prophecy in Delphi was all part of the plan to found and build a sanctuary there, as the young Apollo had announced while still in Delos (52).[32]

As a finder and a cutter of paths, Apollo behaved as a master of the roads, an *aguieus*, and as one who also possessed the art of clearing land. He had found his way through the great primeval forest covering the site of the future Thebes, where "there were no tracks or paths" (225–228). The Athenian tradition was also to associate land clearance with Apollo. The shortest route for Apollo to reach Delphi was bound to pass through Athens, as Aeschylus maintained in the prologue to the *Eumenides*:

> [Phoebus] grounded his ship at the roadstead of Pallas, then
> made his way to this land and a Parnassian home.
> Deep in respect for his degree, Hephaestus' sons
> conveyed him here, for these are builders of roads and changed
> the wilderness to a land that was no wilderness.[33]

Challenging the tradition of the *Homeric Hymn*, the Athenians unequivocally laid claim to precedence: they were already there when Apollo was born in Delos. To commemorate their pioneering role either in the founding of the sanctuary or in the first link established between the oracle and a Greek city, the proud children of Hephaestus placed men carrying two-headed axes at the head of the official procession sent from Athens to Delphi.[34]

---

30 On the technical precision of the *Hymn*, see Roux 1966. He suggests reading *elassan* rather than *enassan*: *elaunein*, in the sense of 'construct', 'start building'. Constructing foundations, laying the threshold stone, assembling walls for the *naos*, using cut stones: all these activities reflect the prime importance of the work of the architect. On Trophonius, cf. Petre 1979.

31 *ktistoisin laessin.* Stones cut by master masons working on the skilled construction of stone walls, rather than walls made from unfired bricks, set on top of stone foundations, as was customary for many buildings in Ephesus, Samos, and Olympia in the seventh century BCE. Cf. Roux 1966:1–5.

32 At this point, it is Leto who is speaking; at 76, Delos repeats the words, and again at 80–81. Apollo himself pronounces them at 247–248 and at 287.

33 Aeschylus *Eumenides* 10–14. Richmond Lattimore's translation.

34 *Scholia to the Eumenides* 13. The *keleuthopoioi* Athenians carried *pelekeis*, two-headed axes made by Hephaestus.

The "Pythais"—decreed by the appearance of a sudden flash of lightning in the sky—set out from the courtyard of the sanctuary of Pythian Apollo on the bank of the Ilissus and proceeded to Delphi by way of Eleusis and the Cithaeron road.[35] This, it was claimed, was the route earlier followed by the future Pythian god. The two-headed axes carried by Apollo's first companions testified to the violence of the effort required to tame the wild space, civilize it, and lay foundations there.

There is one verb of action that links together all the feats performed by Apollo since he took his very first steps: *ktizein*.[36] This is the major term used for "foundation," particularly the foundation of new cities, throughout the colonization of the western territories and the shores of the Black Sea, from the eighth century BCE onward. *Ktizein* operates on a double register: on the one hand it means to clear land, cultivate, tame; on the other, to construct, build, found. According to the Mycenean Linear B tablets, the predominant sense of terms derived from the radical *kti-* was 'to clear, to prepare the ground, to sow, to plant'. The next documentation that we possess, from the eighth century, consisting of the Homeric poems, also testifies both to the sense of 'to found, to construct' and to that of 'to clear land, to cultivate'.[37]

Land that is cleared and set in order becomes a domesticated precinct or a plantation: a well-tended (*euktimenos*) orchard, or a vineyard with neat rows of vines.[38] The same goes for any island or territory as soon as tilled fields transform the landscape, replacing the wild, uncultivated expanses where carnivorous beasts roam.[39] In contrast to the Cyclopes, who are godless, lawless brutes, wherever "eaters of bread" (the human race) settle, they immediately proceed to adapt the place for cultivation. What seems to be a natural impulse prompts them to clear the land, adapt it, and there create fields, orchards, houses, streets, and towns. All these activities are associated with *ktizein*, with whatever is well established, carefully designed, or handsomely constructed.[40] No distinction is made between town planning and the organization of fields and vineyards. Both are part of the same process, a process in which mythological and epic narratives were to distinguish a succession of stages.

---

35 Roux 1976 174–175.
36 This verb, along with *oikizein*, is at the heart of the semantic investigation by Casevitz 1985.
37 Ibid., 21–30.
38 Ibid., 22.
39 Ibid., 23–24.
40 Including "paths" or streets, despite Casevitz's surprise (ibid., 23).

In epic memory, two great cities in particular were associated with the actions involved in the foundation of a town and territory: Thebes and Troy. Thebes of the Seven Gates, the city which, in the *Hymn to Apollo*, has not yet risen from the ground, played a pioneering role: the twins Amphion and Zethus "prepared the site (*hedos ktizein*), laid out the foundations and built the ramparts (*purgos*)."[41] The construction of the gates, the walls, and the main precinct followed hard upon the preparation of the site and the clearance of the territory around it. It was the Dioscuri of Thebes who, with considerable boldness, thus showed the way to build a city at the dawn of this age of civilization.[42] On the Trojan side, the task was divided between three master builders. Dardanus, descended from Zeus, founded (*ktizein*) Dardania; Ilus, the eponymous founder of Ilium, built the town (*polin polizein*),[43] while Poseidon, along with Apollo, under the reign of the unjust Laomedon, surrounded the city with a huge wall designed to render it impregnable.[44]

Every "founded" or "well-founded" (*euktimenos*) city was also a cleared territory, a land put under cultivation, a domesticated, civilized space transformed from its initially wild state. In his *Inquiries*, better known as *Histories*, Herodotus of Halicarnassus tells his Athenian audience, which was passionately keen on autochthony, many tales of the adventures of founding expeditions, of those who boldly, and in some cases rashly, went off to colonize, crossing unknown lands and seas, in order to found new cities that were destined to become great and powerful, in some cases too powerful.[45] For four centuries, the verb *ktizein* was to cover the whole gamut of civilizing activities, from the first efforts to clear a path, through to the city founder's construction of architectural monuments.

In the *Homeric Hymn* in which we have been following his progress, Apollo the Clearer of Land eventually succeeds in founding a sanctuary on the site at Delphi. But nothing about this oracular sanctuary yet indicates the god's future activity as a patron of foundations in general or the extreme

---

41 According to the *Odyssey* ix 262–265, and it alone, at a semantic level.

42 As does Nausithoos, in even more exemplary fashion: *Odyssey* vi 4–10.

43 *Iliad* XX 215–218. There is a distinction between *ktizein* and *polin polizein* (in the sense of building a town within its limits, cf. Casevitz 1985:251–253.

44 *Iliad* VII 452–453. A division of labor, with the building of the wall. Here *polizein*; further on, *Iliad* XXI 441–457, mentions constructing (*demein*) a city wall (*teikhos*) around the town. Poseidon talks of this as though he is working on his own at this task, when speaking of his sufferings in captivity with Apollo.

45 Cf. Malkin 1987. On the imprudence of "anyone who does not abide by any customs": Herodotus 5.42.2 (Dorieus).

delight that he will take in founding a whole succession of cities. The notion of *ktizein* surfaces twice in the *Hymn*, both times in discreet fashion. It first appears in connection with Delos, the island that offers Leto hospitality. It is suggested when the birth of Apollo seems imminent and Delos has just heard Leto promise, by a great oath to the gods, that the island is to become the home, the "base" (51) where Zeus' son means to set the foundations of a temple to which offerings will converge from all over the world. At this point, Delos is called "well founded" (*euktimenê*, 102),[46] since it is the base where it has been decided that Apollo will set up his home. The second allusion to the idea of *ktizein* is even more discreet. It is suggested by the quality of the material chosen for the construction of the first temple at Delphi: the masons at work on the building site use "chiseled" (*ktistoi*) stone, as befits a building of great worth (298).[47] Each of these stonemasons thus contributes to the excellence of this "foundation" and its construction.

At this point though, the clearer of land continues on his way, for at this early stage of his existence, Apollo is still engaged in his travels "over hill and dale." As *Aguieus* in action, Apollo presides over *aguia* and the entire semantic field surrounding the verb *agein* 'to lead, to guide'. *Agos* is the word for a leader, a chief,[48] and *aguia*, the past participle of *agein*, seems to mean 'a path that goes somewhere', a passageway, a way through, a route that leads from one point to another.[49] Apollo *Aguieus*, associated with the building of towns, would stand at the door of a house, a temple entrance, or a city gate. He would be represented there by an altar or a conical stone embodying the god, giving him a form.[50] As ancient glosses point out, the material object is the god himself, but fixed in a static position, at rest here within a space of movement.[51]

---

46 *euktimenê . . . nêsos.* Callimachus' *Hymn to Delos* contrasts the wandering of the island known as Asteria to the rooting of Delos in the sea at the time of Apollo's birth (34–35, 51–54).

47 Stones so well cut and chiselled that Trophonius, the best "stonecutter" (*lithoxoos*) is at the center of a number of Boeotian stories about blocks of stone that could be moved smoothly as though on invisible hinges. Cf. Roux 1966:4–5.

48 *Iliad* XIII 221; 259; 274.

49 Chantraine s.v. *aguieus.* Unreduplicated past participle, according to Chantraine. On "roads" (at the level of semantics and history), see the essential study by Curtius 1894. On representations of roads in archaic thought, cf. Becker 1937.

50 Hesychius, s.v. *aguieus. Bômos*, 'altar'; in the form of a pillar or column, *kiôn. Aguieus bômos*, the *aguieus*-altar or altar-*aguieus* in Sophocles *Laocoon* fr. 370 St. Radt. In the *Homeric Hymn to Apollo*, Phoebus is delighted by the sight of the Ionians gathering on the *aguiai* and setting up the *agôn* (154–155).

51 Photius Berolinensis 25, 26 Reitzenstein: *ho pro tôn auleiôn thurôn kônoeidês kiôn, hieros*

The *Iliad*, which preceded the *Homeric Hymn* that tells the story of Delos and Delphi, describes Apollo operating in space in a more technological fashion than when he forges a path through the woods surrounding the future Thebes. Zeus' plan requires that Apollo play a part in the war: the Trojans must keep up their pressure, the Achaeans must be assailed by fear of the enemy reaching the ramparts built around their camp. Apollo seeks out Hector, his protégé, who has just taken a nasty knock in a skirmish. He comes "up to him,"[52] promises to help him, inspires him with a great anger, and explains what he, Apollo, is now about to do: "I will go ahead of them, making the whole way smooth for their horses' feet" (*proparoithe kiôn ... keleuthon pasan leianeô*).[53] Stepping forward, Apollo then effortlessly flattens the embankment, toppling it into the moat and thereby creating a bridge over it, a long, wide causeway.[54] It is a divine kick that the island Delos has already had cause to evoke when welcoming Leto to its shores, in its fear that the proud Apollo might with a single kick dispatch such a humble island to the bottom of the sea (70–79). From the time of the *Iliad* on, Apollo is constantly demonstrating the force of his foot: he opens up before him a path as "wide as the space that a man covers with a spear-cast, when he is testing his strength."[55] There was really no need to involve the axes of the Athenian land clearers. With a single kick, Apollo opens up a path, makes a road, scorning all obstacles: "He knocked down the Achaean wall like a boy at the seaside playing childish games with the sand, building a castle to amuse himself and then, with his hands and feet, destroying the whole work for fun."[56]

In the *Iliad*, there are some walls that deserve to be destroyed, and Apollo flattens those of the Achaeans with all the greater assurance given that, when the Greeks dug the moat and built the ramparts, they forgot to offer the customary sacrifices to the appropriate gods. Poseidon had already lodged a complaint about this in terms so bitter that Zeus had felt obliged to promise his brother that one day soon the sea, with a single faultless wave, would obliterate all trace of the impious walls in question.[57] For now, though, Poseidon was biding his time. It was Apollo's turn.

Apollônos, kai autos ho theos.

52 *Iliad* XV 247 (*antên*). Translations from the *Iliad* are by E. V. Rieu.

53 *Iliad* XV 261–262. *Leianeô* 'to flatten, soften', but also to crush in a mortar or with one's teeth.

54 *Iliad* XV 355–357.

55 *Iliad* XV 357. A "flattener," in the sense of "bulldozer," a word that emphasizes the aspect of Apollo as a god who strikes or flattens the enemy.

56 *Iliad* XV 361–363.

57 *Iliad* VII 455–63.

The footfall of Apollo was certainly terrible. As he had approached the entrance to Olympus, it had made the gods there tremble (1–2). When the Argonauts, dropping with fatigue, landed "at break of day," it was similarly Apollo's step that made the island of Thynia shake.[58] In a single stride, Apollo could reach his goal as surely as an arrow let fly by the best of archers.[59] The minute he appeared in Cyrene, when he manifested himself in the sanctuary there, the chorus greeting him referred to his foot striking the temple door.[60] In Troad, at Smintheus, Strabo claims he saw him stepping on a rat.[61] Apollo reached his goal in a single stride. In the opening lines of the *Iliad* a dark figure is glimpsed. It is Apollo, angry, bending his bow, "and his descent was like nightfall,"[62] a swiftly moving god slipping past to take up position a little way from the ships, his bow at the ready. He appears again as a fleeting figure, in the cultural tradition of the fourth century: Apollo, the civilizing god, roaming the earth, keeping an eye on the human race, dissuading it from partaking of the wild nourishment that is a feature of the parades of Demeter at Triptolemus, in the Sulpician imagery of Eleusis.[63]

In the *Homeric Hymn*, Apollo, the walker and clearer of land, manifests a mode of action that is expressed by the compound verbal forms of the movement denoted by *bainein*.[64] This means 'to go', but not in the sense of to go and come back, nor of to depart; rather, it implies moving from one place to another or, to be more precise, *bainein* seems to mean 'to place the foot firmly', be it embarking or disembarking, scaling town walls or following in someone else's tracks.[65] The gesture of *bainein* also implies a certain static dimension: "setting one's foot" has a static connotation that is conveyed by a series of words derived from the same root: *bêlos* meaning 'threshold'; *bêma* meaning 'tribune', the place to which an orator steps up, to speak; *embas* or *bêla* meaning a 'shoe' or 'sandals'; *bebêlos*, a 'trampled space', sometimes with the sense of 'profane'; and *bebaios*, whatever is 'solid, securely placed'.[66] The first thing that Apollo does is take up a firm stance, stand solidly on his

---

58 Apollonius Rhodius *Argonautica* 2.671–84.
59 Pindar *Pythian* 3.75 (*bamati d'en protoi*).
60 Callimachus *Hymn to Apollo* 3 Williams.
61 Strabo 13, 48. Grégoire, Goossens, and Mathieu 1949.
62 *Iliad* I 47 (*ēie*: used absolutely.).
63 Ephorus, in Strabo 9.3.11–12 (= FGH 70 F 31b Jacoby).
64 Cf. Létoublon 1985. The *Homeric Hymn to Apollo* contains over thirty verbs of movement: fourteen examples of *bainein*; eleven of the *hik-* group; four of the *eimi-erkhomai* series.
65 Létoublon 1985:123–143.
66 Létoublon 1985:133.

two feet. This is the god who solidly supports or "protects" (*amphibainein*) Chryse, in the *Iliad*, and Ismarus in the *Odyssey*.[67] *Amphibainein* can mean to be supported firmly on both sides, as in the case of Apollo providing a base and stability for a town or a territory.

In short, the step of Apollo possesses quite a range of specific characteristics; it passes over a boundary or obstacle; it secures a firm stance on the ground; it solidly establishes the path that it has opened up. His younger brother Hermes, also an excellent walker, has a quite different step. Although he steps over the threshold, away from his mother's house, on the very night of his birth, he soon turns back and returns from his night of plunder, rubbing out his own tracks and reversing the hoof marks of the cattle he has stolen from the herds of the gods kept on the mountains of Pieria.[68] His tricks with footprints certainly succeed in bewildering Apollo when he sets out to track down the audacious thief.

A path trodden by Apollo was characterized by an end and a beginning. It was a path that reached its destination, a way opened up by a god whose every stride fashioned a "well-constructed" route, a path that was *aguia*, firmly cut (*euktimena*).[69] Apollo *Aguieus* presided over the civilizing power that roads and paths possessed in the organization of a territory. It is well known how important this was to Greek cities.[70] In Sparta it was the kings, the two of them, who held jurisdiction over everything to do with "public roads" (*hodoi dêmosiai*).[71] Meanwhile, in Attica, it was the yokers of oxen, the Buzyges, who in their own way exercised a jurisdiction that closely resembled that of the "king" or archon who dealt with defilement resulting from blood shed on the ground: when such defilement occurred, they called down curses, proclaiming the great importance of roads constructed for the protection of "civilized life," a life that also depended on the sharing of water and fire.[72] Just as in the English language roads are "constructed," in Greek they were "cut" (*temnein*).[73] Only barbarians such as the Scythian nomads lived

---

67 *Iliad* I 17 and 451; *Odyssey* ix 198, interpreted by Létoublon 1985:134–143.

68 *Bainein* also occurs frequently in the *Homeric Hymn to Hermes*. Movement and space provide an extremely rich experimental field for studying the differential characteristics of Hermes and Apollo.

69 *Iliad* VI 391: Troy is a town with fine streets, thoroughfares that are "well cut, well constructed" (*hodon . . . euktimenas kat'aguias*). In Delphi the official access to the stadium for the Pythian Games was called *aguia* (cf. Pouilloux 1983).

70 Cf. Curtius 1894:29–37.

71 Herodotus 6.57.

72 Durand 1986:175–193.

73 A number of epigraphical discoveries seem to show that boundary markers and stelae indicating essential distances between various spots used to stand in public places and at

in territories where no roads were "cut."[74] It was altogether in the order of things that a city's land should be subject to such "cutting," and this would be entrusted to experts who were well aware of Apollo's authority in this domain.[75] Moreover, Greek roads were not only "cut" but also "constructed" (*demein, eudmêtos*),[76] just as a tool, a wall, or a dwelling was.

In the version of the *Hymn*, which tells not only of the establishment of an oracle but also of Apollo's decision "to build a glorious temple" on the same spot, once the god reaches the foot of Parnassus, he himself lays the first stone for the foundations of his sanctuary. Apollo is his own architect. Helpers, from the surrounding area, then hurry to assist him: first, the threshold layers, Trophonius and Agamedes, then the stonecutters. The temple of stone is the first to be built. In contrast, in the tradition recorded by Pausanias when he visited Delphi, the temple of stone was the last to be built, after three other kinds of materials had been tried. First there had been a hut of laurel branches, next a construction of wax and wings, then a building of bronze. Apollo remains in the background in that version.[77] The god of the oracle is set apart from the architect god.[78] An architect called *Aguieus*, from the land of Hyperboreans, is claimed to have built Apollo's first temple,[79] although we are not told whether it was made from plaited branches of laurel collected in the valley of Tempe, where Apollo was supposed to have gone to purify himself

---

important crossroads. A stone deciphered by Chandler close to the Acropolis—engraved in the fifth century BCE—informed the passerby that the city had set it up to "signify" (*sêmainein*) to everybody the length (*metron*) of the "distance to be covered" (*odoporia*), in this case the distance between Piraeus and the altar of the Twelve Gods (IG II2 2640). Cf. Salviat and Servais 1964; also the remarks of Curtius 1894:20–25.

74 Herodotus 4.131.

75 Callimachus *Aitia* II F 43.64–65 Pfeiffer.

76 Curtius 1894:25, which describes a late inscription from Syria that features the words *hodon ktizein. Demein, eudmetos* are common in Herodotus 2.124; 7.200. Also in connection with altars.

77 Pausanias 10.5.9–13. Cf. Sourvinou-Inwood 1979. Pindar also believes the temple built with the aid of Trophonius and Agamedes to have been the last one. In the *Iliad* IX 404–405 and in the *Odyssey* viii 79–81, the "stone threshold" (bearing no architect's name) was already a feature of the Apollonian site in Delphi and of its oracle. Sourvinou-Inwood (236–237), discusses the architectural meaning of the Homeric expression.

78 In the traditions echoed by Pindar, Apollo may have been represented as the *arkhitektôn* who drew up the plan and gave the orders rather than the one who executed the project, built it with his own hands (*autokheriei*), as is claimed by the signature-inscription (about 550 BCE) discovered on a temple column in the Granicus area between Cyzicus and Lampsacus (cf. Robert 1950: 78–80).

79 Pausanias 10.5.7 refers to the tradition of Boio, a local woman who was the first to sing in hexameters and whose hymn named the first builders of the temple of Apollo (*khrêsterion . . . ektelein*) Pagasus and Aguieus.

after slaying the Python.[80] The Hyperborean *Aguieus* bears the same name as Apollo the Walker. He arrives accompanied by Pagasus, another Hyperborean,[81] whose name evokes another aspect of Apollo, the god known as *Pagasios*, from Pagasae in Thessaly, from which the expedition of the Argonauts set out.[82] The Apollo suggested by Pagasus was a god of sea voyages: the god who showed Jason the paths of the sea, he was also an angry god.

The road leading to the sanctuary of Delphi was impassable. Swan (*Kuknos*),[83] fathered by Ares, was in the habit of attacking and robbing those taking great hecatombs to Python.[84] This armed Swan waged relentless war on the devotees of Apollo. It was in the temple of the god of Pagasae that Heracles challenged this son of Ares, putting a stop to his murderous activities. Heracles was fighting in the service of Apollo, and the anger of the god of Pagasae was so great that he ordered the river Anaurus, swollen by torrential

---

80 According to the reconstruction of Pindar (*Schol. in Paen VIII*, P. Oxy. 841 F. 87) by Snell 1938, the first temple was built from laurel branches brought from Tempe, as Pausanias himself declares, 10.5.9. Bérard thinks that the temple he discovered in Eretria was this temple of laurel (Cf. Altherr-Charon and Bérard 1980), where Apollo was known as the "laurel-bearer," *Daphnêphoros*, and was the city's poliad deity. On the traditions of the laurel and the laurel temple cf. Sourvinou-Inwood 1979 233–238n77. There is no good reason to reject the idea of Apollo himself "plaiting" together his first laurel temple (as Altherr-Charon and Bérard do, 239), on the model of Apollo constructing an altar in Delos made from intertwined horns (*plekein, huphainein, pêgnunai*, in Callimachus, *Hymn to Apollo* 61–62 Williams). However, this is nowhere explicitly attested.

81 A number of prophets and ministers of Apollo came from the land of the Hyperboreans, as did offerings brought by Virgins and Youths, Leto, and Eilithye and, above all, Apollo himself, who regularly went there to attend sacrifices in his honor. The religious relations between the land of the Hyperboreans and Delos are clearly attested, notably by historical evidence provided by epigraphical studies of fourth-century BCE Delos: Tréheux 1953. According to Tréheux, these offerings (straw and sacred sheafs of corn) were brought by an unknown people connected with the Delian cult of Apollo: "Some isolated group of Ionians living somewhere on the borders beyond Scythia" (764). The offerings consisted of the first fruits of the harvest and were abrought by the Hyperborean virgins and youths, initially five in number, known as the *Perpherées* (Herodotus 4.33–35, and the analyses of Bruneau 38–48).

82 Pagasae where there was a sanctuary of Apollo. It was on the altar of Apollo *Embasios* (the Apollo of embarkations) that Jason offered up a sacrifice, reminding the Argonauts of Apollo's promise "to reveal the paths of the sea" to them (Apollonius Rhodius *Argonautica* 1.359–61).

83 Cf. the data collected by Krappe 1942 (leaving aside the etymologies and interpretations amassed by Krappe in a series of related essays); also Vian 1945.

84 [Hesiod] *Shield* 58 ff. This figure had a very bad reputation: he murdered strangers and even built himself a temple with the skulls of his victims, a temple for Apollo. Swan-Kuknos was also associated with Apollo through his winged form and the power of his voice. See the extremely thorough analysis by Janko 1986.

rain, to sweep away all trace of the tomb built in honor of Swan by his follow-ers.[85] Pagasus, the companion of Aguieus and the second architect from the land of the Hyperboreans, is perhaps intended to convey, through the tales of Pagasae, a reminder of how hateful and fatal is the presumption of those who thwart the right of routes to be freely used and trodden by all who respect Apollo *Aguieus* and his network of paths that link houses, sanctuaries, and cities throughout the civilized world.[86]

According to Pindar, who knew what he was talking about, the Hyperboreans were distant and mysterious: "And traveling neither by ships nor on foot could you find the marvelous way to the assembly of the Hyperboreans."[87] The Hyperboreans were inaccessible—whereas all roads led to Delphi—and not only did they produce architects but they were also given to following the long roads and paths taken by processions.[88] They carried ceremonial offerings over long distances and, by reason of their long travels along sacred ways, mythically they came to symbolize the routes known as "Pythian," "Daphnephoric" or—rather less commonly—"lithophoric."[89] However, in that the offerings that they carried consisted of conical or square stones rather than straw, sheaves of wheat, and laurel branches, the Hyperboreans seem somewhat out of step with the other sacred processions that passed along these routes.

In Miletus, in the heart of Ionia, a brotherhood known as "the Singers" (*Molpoi*)[90] exercised a partly political, partly religious power within the sphere of the poliad god, Apollo *Delphinios*. Toward the end of the sixth century BCE, each year, when spring returned and with it Apollo, a procession would set out from Miletus for Didyma.[91] It followed a route marked out by a whole string of toponyms, sanctuaries, and other proper names. The journey was

---

85 [Hesiod] *Shield* 471–479.
86 Curtius (1894:32–40) made a study of this network of sacred paths linking the various sanc-tuaries of Apollo; access routes, commercial routes, paths taken by temple officials. The path to Delphi, for example, was placed under the protection of the Amphictyonians.
87 Pindar, *Pythian* 10.30. William H. Race's translation.
88 For example, Abaris, the prophet of Apollo; cf. Delcourt 1955:158, 161, 163; Bolton 1962:156–158.
89 A *lithophoros*, or stone-bearing priest is mentioned in an epigraphic document from Eleusis (see note 99).
90 Apart from the bibliography provided by Sokolowski 1955, no. 50, see Graf 1974 and 1979. Also the analyses by Georgoudi 1986.
91 Sokolowski 1955. The Molpoi recorded in writing the ceremonies and rituals carried out in honor of Apollo at fixed dates: they organized the *orgia*, the rituals that they carried out as *orgiônes*. The Cretan priests established in Delphi by Apollo did likewise.

punctuated by special songs and sacrifices. Members of the Molpoi brotherhood carried along two stones known as *gulloi*.[92] The first was set up close to Hecate, "the Hecate standing at the gates" at the entrance to the city.[93] This *gullos*-stone was crowned and anointed with pure wine, in honor of the deity who possessed an altar within the shelter of the sanctuary of Apollo of Miletus.[94] Seventeen kilometers further on, the second stone was deposited before the gates of the sanctuary of Apollo at Didyma.[95]

These conical or rectangular stone *gulloi* probably took the form of pillars similar to those that embodied the presence of Apollo *Aguieus*, the deity of the roads and paths that led from one place to another. Used as altar stones, they marked out the route linking two temples of Apollo, the sacred way taken by the priests of the *Delphinios*, who officiated at the ceremonies or *orgia* described on the stele. These stone *gulloi* that were carried the whole way along the Apollonian route, from one end to the other, represented the *aguieus* god, the very one that Pausanias noticed, in rectangular form, in Megalopolis[96] and also, in conical form, standing above the path opened up by Battus of Cyrene, at the spot where this reached the entrance to the sanctuary raised in honor of Apollo, the deity of foundations (*Arkhêgetês*), who had himself helped Battus the Stammerer to found the city.[97]

These stones came in a wide variety of shapes. Whether as roadside milestones, altar stelae in transit, or monumental cones deposited at the entrance to some sanctuary,[98] they all testified to the powers of Aguieus the Architect, who followed in the footsteps of Apollo so as at last to reach the site of the Delphic oracle. Whether known as Aguieus or as Pagasus, Apollo's architect operated as a builder, but also, in a more ritual fashion, as a *lithophoros*, a bearer of stones whose first task was to create "well built" and "solidly constructed" thoroughfares in the manner of Apollo. An echo of these *lith-*

---

92 L. 25. Cf. Hesychius, s.v. *gulloi*, and Kraus 1960:12–13.

93 Kraus 1960:13, 63, 70, 107.

94 Hecate in the precinct (*entemenios*) of Apollo *Delphinios*. An altar to her has been found in the sanctuary of Apollo at Miletus, cf. Kraus 1960:11.

95 Sokolowski 1955, 1.26–27. Cf. Schneider 1987.

96 *Skhêma tetragonon*, Pausanias 8.32.4.

97 Cf. Balestrazzi 1980–81.

98 Apollo's relationship with uncut stones has fascinated a whole string of interpreters who have believed they could both resolve the original etymology of Apollo and seize upon the transition from aniconical representation to anthropomorphism, cf. e.g. Solders 1935. In the Orphic tradition, Apollo presented Helenus with a speaking stone that prophecied the fall of Troy (Schamp 1981).

ophoroi seems detectable in the college of the *semiophoroi* or Bearers of Signs, who were the companions of Apollo the Founder at Hierapolis in Phrygia.[99]

Roads, roadside altars, sanctuaries, temples with altars, gates, and walls are all constructions befitting a god who, as he took his very first steps, had announced that he wished "to make a dwelling" (*oikia thesthai*, 46)[100] and who, on his long march, more than once declared: "This is where I intend to build a glorious temple." Apollo displayed an innate taste for monumental constructions. In the *Iliad*, his humiliated priest, praying to him as he proceeds along the beach, bearing the god's scepter and wearing his ornaments,[101] testifies to the care he has always lavished upon the dwellings of Apollo: "if ever I raised a roof for a shrine that delighted you, if ever I burnt you the fat thighs of a bull or a goat."[102] The roof constructed by Chryses may not have been fashioned from the indestructible beams of cypress wood that the Alcmeonids presented to the god of Delphi with a level of pomp and ceremony that the Greek world would never forget; but it would at least have been the kind of highly finished roof that one from time to time finds commemorated in archaic dedications.[103] In Thessaly, on a stele dating from about 550 BCE, two characters claimed the credit for constructing a roof: the one for setting it in place; the other for assembling it, which probably meant bolting its rafters together.[104] Meanwhile, in the Granicus region, midway between Cyzicus and Lampsacus, another dedication, carved in the fluting of an Ionic pillar, commemorated the fact that somebody (who remains anonymous, on account of a break in the stone) had made a covering for a sanctuary, aided—it is true—by his companions, who paid the costs out of the temple's income and the proceeds collected from the sale of the pelts of sacrificial victims.[105]

---

99 Judeich 1898:119–120, no. 153: *sêmiaphoroi tou Arkhêgetou Apollônos*. Cf. Ritti 1985:108–109. Apollo is present in the micropantheon mentioned in the decree in honor of the torch bearer Themistocles, a high dignitary of Eleusis: Roussel 1934. Alongside *Patrôos*, the priest of Hermes, stands the Herald (*kêrux*) of Pythian Apollo. Next comes the *Lithophoros* who is also the priest of Zeus Horios, Athena *Horia* and Poseidon *Prosbaterios* and *Themelioukhos*. Moreover, the stone carried by the *Lithophoros* is the "sacred stone" (*hieros lithos*).

100 At this point it is Leto who makes the announcement.

101 *Iliad* I 14: *stemmata*. The *stemmata* were the ribbons that adorned Apollo's "cult statue," and that also made him impressively present in the person of his priest (according to the interpretation of Servais 1967).

102 *Iliad* I 39 (Loeb translation adapted). *Erephein* 'to cover'; *orophos* or *orophê* 'roof, covering'.

103 Pindar *Pythian* 5.42–46. Cf. Roux 1979:208–215.

104 *SEG* XVII 287 and the analyses of Masson. The verb *teukhein* is here associated with another verb, *krounein*, meaning "to fix with nails or bolts" (attested for *epikrounein*: Masson 1967:101–102).

105 Published in Robert 1950:78–80. The verb here is *poiein*, used both for *neôn* 'temple', and for

---

Apollo's many temples boast not only high rafters and impressive roofs, but also large and imposing thresholds, made of a single slab of stone, no doubt very like the one set in place by Trophonius and Agamedes.[106] The threshold was the largest stone in the whole building and it was "around the threshold" that the stonemasons then proceeded to construct the temple walls. A threshold could be as much as six meters long and two wide and might weigh about ten tons,[107] as did that of the fourth-century temple at Delphi itself. It is the most frequently mentioned part of Apollonian temples. Agamemnon stepped across the threshold when he came to consult the oracle, as Demodocus recalls in the palace of the Phaeacians.[108] When Croesus is set free, it is upon the threshold of Apollo that he lays down the chains of his bondage.[109] It was on the threshold too, that suppliant murderers would sit, awaiting the coming of the god of Cyrene.[110] The archaic words used for threshold reflect two aspects of Apollo's behavior: *houdos* refers to the firm support upon which the architect was to base his building; *bêlos* conveys the imprint of the foot placed there, ensuring a steady stance.[111]

Walls and cities belong to the domain of the Apollo who declares himself to be a founder and creator of cities. But, to look no further than the setting in which the *Homeric Hymn* begins, the first architectural forms that Apollo brings into being in his wake are altars. In her very first words, designed to elicit the island's hospitality, Leto refers to altars. Delos alone will be known for the fragrant altars set all around Apollo's home: "All men will bring you hecatombs and gather here and incessant savor of rich sacrifice will always arise" (57–58). Leto makes Delos a solemn promise: "Phoebus shall have here his fragrant altar and precinct" (87–88). Yet Leto can do nothing to alter the fact that, however indissociable from Apollo the place where he lives may be, equally so is the impulse that carries him away from it.

---

stegê 'roof'. Only the name of the "architect" survives: Leucippus, who himself worked on the construction of the temple, *autokheriei*, with his own hands.

106 Out of the thirty examples of *naos* 'temple' in the *Homeric Hymns*, twenty-one appear in the *Hymn to Apollo*.

107 I am here following data provided by Roux 1966.

108 *Odyssey* viii 74. When the riches of Apollo of Delphi are evoked at *Iliad* IX 404, it is again the "threshold" (*oudos*) that represents the temple.

109 Herodotus 1.90.

110 Sokolowski 1962, no. 115, B 52.

111 Hellmann 1988:245.

The first step in his travels was Telphusa, where Apollo conceived the plan of establishing an oracle and an altar that was as "well built" (*eudmêtos*, 271) as a well-cut road or path. The site's jealousy put an end to the idea, but later Apollo was to return there to confound the site of Telphusa by building himself a sacred altar smack in the middle of the sacred wood, close to the spring. Before that altar, all would hail him as the Apollo of Telphusa, so that the humiliation of the jealous nymph would never be forgotten (384). Once Apollo had reached Crisa and built his temple there, those altars were indeed constructed, and they did attract showers of sacrificial offerings (289), just as Leto had promised when she declared "incessant savor of rich sacrifice will always arise" (57–58).[112] A well-designed altar testified to the skill of its founder. At this table and in this precinct Apollo, always partial to sacrificial victims, proceeded to organize the first sacrifice, with the cult's own officiating priests and instruments and all its own rituals. It was an inaugural scene that did justice to a god explicitly recognized—later, but with retroactive force[113]—as the highest of all patrons of "consecrations" (*hidruseis*), that is to say, of the founding of cults, festivals, and sacrifices throughout the entire Greek world.

Contemplating his oracular sanctuary, Apollo paused to consider: who could he bring there to officiate as *orgiônes* (389–390) for his Pythian cult? The forests through which he had passed and the lands that he had crossed had been deserted, with no sign of human inhabitants. The only people glimpsed, in the distance, had been Phlegyae, consumed by an insane pride. He would have to look elsewhere, out to sea: there, a ship appeared, carrying Cretans from Cnossos. These would be the ministers of his cult and would perform the sacrifices (*hiera . . . rhezein*) and make known the *themistes*, the "founding words of the oracle" (393–395). No sooner had he come to this decision than Apollo assumed the form of a dolphin and leaped up on to the ship's bridge. The crew was breathless with surprise at this marvel (400–406). The great dolphin steered the ship (421), with the wind blowing it ahead on a trajectory that defied the common sense of nautical lore (421–437). When Crisa hove into view, Apollo rose up, shining like a star. Flames caught in the sanctuary's fires, and he made his way in through a double row of tripods. The people of Crisa, suddenly thronging the sacred way, were terrified. With the shrill cries of an *ololugê*, the women and girls greeted this manifestation of Apollo

---

112 Returning to the initial promise made by Leto.
113 That of Plato *Republic* 427b6–7.

(440–447). Their cries heralded the sacrifice and killings that were soon to take place amid the tripods.[114]

Already Apollo was busy. He welcomed the strangers who had come there by "watery paths" and invited them to disembark, *ekbainein* (451–457).[115] Then he told them what to do: "Light fire upon the altar" (*pur epikaiein*); "make an offering of white meal" (*alphita leuka thuein*); "next, stand side by side around the altar and pray" (*eukhesthai ... paristamenoi peri bômôn*, 490–492). This was the first altar to be used. It needed a name: "In as much as ... I sprang upon the swift ship in the form of a dolphin (*delphinos*), pray to me as Apollo Delphinus; also, the altar itself shall be called Delphinus and [visible] and overlooking for ever" (495–496).[116] His last advice to his future ministers was to "sup and pour an offering to the blessed gods who dwell on Olympus. [Then, having eaten,] come with me, singing the hymn *Iê* Paean, until you come to the place where you shall keep my rich temple" (458).[117]

Apollo had spoken. The Cretans knew what they had to do. Now it was up to them, and they followed Apollo's instructions to the letter: they built an altar, made the first sacrifice, gave a name to the god of the territory, and then dined together without forgetting libations for the Olympians (502–512). It was an inaugural moment for the human race, which was making its first appearance in the territory that Apollo had prepared. The scene for the sacrifice was already set: materials for the altar were ready; the wood for the fire awaited; the cereal grain was there. No inventiveness was required, either for lighting the fire or for finding the cereals.[118] All the necessary instruments and ingredients were to hand, concomitant with Apollo's declared desire to see "the rites performed" (*hiera rhezein*, 394). Those responsible for performing the rites immediately set to work, completing in the correct order all the operations listed by their host. Then, having eaten, the Cretans set off, headed by the "prancing, high-stepping Apollo," playing his lyre (514–516).[119]

---

114 Cf. Gernet 1932.
115 Apollo is very much concerned with landings and altars set up on the seashore, on the boundary of a territory.
116 *Epopsios*, 'visible', but also all-seeing.
117 Apollo knows the law of "men who are eaters of bread." He accordingly invites them to eat their fill, 497–98.
118 This stands in contrast to the first sacrifices performed by Hermes, who had to rub two sticks together in order to produce the spark of a technological fire: *Hymn to Hermes* 108–142, together with the interpretations of Kahn 1978:50–56.
119 The same "fine, prancing step" as in his expedition to Olympus (203). *Arkhein* in the sense of leading the way, being in charge.

On that seashore altar there had been no suggestion of any blood sacrifice of animals. The time for hecatombs and "rich smoke" offered up to the god would come later. In that first ritual the offering had consisted of cereals consumed directly by the fire on the altar, a pure altar fed by barley grain that was not shared by those officiating. The Cretans dined separately among themselves, not forgetting to pour a libation for the gods. However, at the Delphic site, in front of, if not inside the temple of Pythian Apollo, the ministers from Crete were to perform sacrifices of a quite different nature. Just as they were wondering what kind of life awaited them in this rocky place bereft of vines or pastureland, Apollo gave them new orders, telling them: "Though each of you with knife in hand should slaughter (*sphazein*) sheep continually, yet would you always have abundant store" (535–536). Here were the promised hecatombs, the savors of meat, the pleasures of sacrificing rich victims drawn there by the centripetal force of this second altar, constructed at the same time as the temple was set upon its vast foundations. Furthermore, in this second sacrificial scene, the principal agent was no longer the "visible" (*epopsios*) altar fire, but a sacrificial knife, deployed openly rather than being concealed, as was customary, in a basket, hidden by the cereal grain. The bloody knife was here allowed full visibility, for Apollo sanctioned it with solemn violence.

Those two altars in the Apollonian Delphic landscape stood in contrast to each other by virtue of the manner of their inauguration. There were two other Apollonian altars that were similarly opposed in Delos, which had no oracle but was nevertheless rich in altars and sacrificial offerings. In Delos, in particular, Apollo reigned over an altar that was famous for the simple, natural offerings brought to it from every side. This Apollo, known as *Genetôr*, received on his table only "the pure fruits of the earth": barley and cakes; mallow and asphodel.[120] It was said that this was the altar to which Pythagoras came, to do homage to the god beloved above all others.[121] No animal sacrifices were ever made here, for it was a "pure" altar, untouched by blood. But it was situated "behind" another,[122] known as *Keratôn*, which was an altar of horns, constructed by Delian Apollo from the interwoven horns of goats and fed by sacrifices of the most bloody kind.[123]

---

120 Cf. Bruneau 1970:161–165.
121 Cf. Detienne 1994a:55–59.
122 The location of this altar remains uncertain, despite the hypotheses and research of archaeologists (Bruneau 1970:163 and 510).
123 On the altar of horns, see Bruneau 1970:19–29. It was an altar covered by a roof, but it has

The *Homeric Hymn* presents us with one last image, at the end of the road from Delos: positioned before the altar of his magnificent temple, the god promises his ministers that in the right hand of each there will always be a sacrificial knife. This final violent note echoes two from the beginning of the *Hymn*. The first was that struck by the demeanor of the young god as he burst into Olympus with his bow at the ready, in the full force of his anger (4–6). It was a hint of violence that the text then repeats and amplifies when Delos confesses its fears to Leto: "They say that Apollo will be one that is very haughty and *will greatly lord it* among gods and men" (180). The meaning of *atasthalos* is 'one with a limitless pride', like the Titans who tried to oppose heaven and stand up to Zeus; and *prutane* means 'one who domineers', always determined to impose his own will. He was certainly a violent god, this walker and builder of altars and temples who came to install himself on the heights above Crisa.

---

not been found by the archaeologists working on Delos. Discoveries at Dreros in Crete have revealed the design of another such altar (24).

3

Forgetting Delphi Between Apollo and Dionysus[*]

L ET US BE CLEAR WHO is at fault if we are still today attracted and fascinated
   by the opposition between Apollonian and Dionysian, be it in a Poussin
   painting or at the origins of Greek religion. It is certainly not the fault of
Orpheus' first disciples, who did make use of the contrasts between Dionysus
and Apollo, their master, but left behind them only fragments having no effect
on the Greeks' religious discourse.[1] Nor have we cause to blame the theologian
from Delphi, Plutarch, Hadrian's contemporary, who, while discoursing on the
Delphic *epsilon* (that mysterious offering in the form of a letter or number),
made use of speculations of other "theologians," alternating, according to a
Heraclitean paradigm, the poles of Apollo and Dionysus in the coming-to-be
of the world, in which may be read the contrasts between rhythms, musical
forms, and characters distinct to each one of these two powers.[2]

All evidence points to one guilty party: Friederich Nietzsche, intoxicating
himself with the rich dialectic of this contrast, quite free of any reference to
Delphi or more local versions, about which he could not care less. Some twenty
years after *The Birth of Tragedy*, which he had so generously defended against
Ulrich von Wilamowitz-Möllendorff, prince of the philistines and philologists,[3]
Erwin Rohde writes not a single footnote alluding to the Nietzschean variations when he composes *Psyche* (1894), although he writes a complete account
of how the union of Apollo with Dionysus (who has "become Greek") took
place in Delphi, and nowhere else.[4]

---

[*] Originally published in *Classical Philology* 96 (2001) 147–158.

1 Detienne 1985b. Cf. Detienne 1989b:116–132.

2 Cf. Plutarch *De E Apud Delphos* 9 (388e–389e). In a conference organized at Johns Hopkins
  University by the Department of Classical Studies (October 1993) entitled "Apollo and
  Dionysus: Genealogy of a Fascination," Giulia Sissa presented a new Heraclitean reading of
  this passage of Plutarch and its relation to certain aphorisms of Nietzsche.

3 Gründer 1969; Dixsaut 1995.

4 Rohde 1925:282–303. A union at the highest level, and for Rohde essential to the history of
  Greek religion.

So let us forget Delphi, forget Nietzsche, no matter how pleasurable it may be to watch his drunken, voluptuous antics with the Dionysian sublimating the Apollonian.[5] The byways have their own charms, even if they lead neither to a quintessential opposition, nor to the secret truth of a Panhellenic oracle. Our purpose here is simply to effect an archaeology of the practices of polytheism, from one site to another, throughout the whole of Greece, noting as many configurations as possible associating Apollo with Dionysus—and with other not-necessarily-insignificant powers as well. Nor will we neglect groupings, that is, micropantheons, in which Apollo and Dionysus are coupled, playing in concert, or practicing singular exchanges. This recourse to the byways is indeed an exploration of the practices of polytheism at their most concrete.[6]

In a system of multiple gods, in Greece as elsewhere, as soon as there are altars, sanctuaries, stories, and spontaneously "theological" speech, one notes groupings of gods, recurring associations, regular hierarchies, and others more unusual. A polytheistic system is primarily constituted by the relations between gods—oppositions, antithetic or complementary figures of three, four, or five elements. From the outset, practices come to light in relations, and even in a system of relations. We emphasize practices and their variety in order to foreground concrete configurations and groups of powers, that is to say, the acts, objects, and situations that contextualize the relations between divinities. The advantage of this approach is twofold: on the one hand, it allows us to do away with the model—so harmful in the case of Apollo or Dionysus—of a god always endowed with a specific "mode of action" as soon as we see him as dominant. Paradoxically, this model was inspired by Georges Dumézil and condemned us to building static pantheons inhabited by agent-gods, individually specified according to a way of acting that was unique and constant. Another advantage to our empirical and concrete approach is that it gives access to the procedures that uncover the production of distinct powers—powers no longer (or not to be) hypostasized as (or in) gods, or abstracted and converted into their singular attributes (for example, Dionysus god of wine and *mania*, and so on).

Furthermore, this approach has an experimental dimension somewhat analogous to qualitative analysis in chemistry. Rather than accepting the first conventional idea of such and such a power, the analyst can be attentive first

---

5 Haar 1993:221–273, "La Joie tragique," is to be read above all.
6 I have treated this form of analysis more extensively in "Experimenting in the Field of Polytheisms" (reprinted in Part 2, Chapter 1 of the present volume), and have shown its interest in Detienne 1998a.

to the objects, the acts, the particular situations presented by the primary data, using these as so many catalysts to see what aspect of this particular divine power comes to the surface in the given configuration. Prolonging the experiment, the analyst will submit the various powers associated or contrasting with the first power to the same catalysts, first in the initial configuration, then in those connected with it. Sometimes a detail—some gesture, object, or situation—from some far province or hidden corner will bring out the place in the system of some seemingly alien aspect of the power under observation. Thus the experiment identifies a range of possibilities, without which polytheism remains opaque, a dead system.

Of all the couples of Greek mythology, that of Apollo and Dionysus is the most famous, at least in the post-Nietzschean era. Paradoxically, the more (following Rohde's *Psyche*) Apollonian versus Dionysian became an accepted contrast, the greater the historians' and philologists' indifference toward them, in a profession intimidated by the Germans. Historians of Greek religion, be they English, Italian, Spanish, German, or French, pass by this issue very quickly, particularly since Delphi proposes so many unsolved and discouraging problems: Aeschylus, placing himself at Delphi, points to a Corycian cave with Dionysus the Noisy (*Bromios*) arrived from Thebes, but when and how?[7] Antiquarians of the fourth and third centuries tell of Dionysus buried in Apollo's temple next to the omphalos and the tripod; does he never pronounce an oracle, not even by incubation?

One needs only to step away from the well-trodden path to Delphi to find a series of sites (I count twenty so far) where Apollo and Dionysus are coupled, sometimes strongly contrasted, and sometimes trading instruments or setting, occasionally accomplishing complete exchange between themselves. It will be enough here to present two or three of these in order to reveal the complexity of the relations between Apollo and Dionysus, as well as to exemplify in their pleasant company our experimental procedures.

Icarion's Accomplices

Let us begin in Icarion, an ancient village in Attica, known as Dionyso today. It is here that one of the oldest encounters between Apollo and Dionysus takes place. Situated on the edge of Athens, Icarion is also the home of Thespis,

---

7 Eventually, a complete survey by a competent scholar will appear. For the moment, two examples: Jeanmaire 1978:187–198; Burkert 1985:223–225. Certain analyses, nevertheless, offer extremely rich material for working on complex materials already uncovered. I am thinking, on the one hand, of Calame 1990:289–396, and, on the other, of Brulé 1987.

the first tragic author: he invents the actor and the mask, and is triumphant at the Great Dionysia of Athens, between 536 and 533 BCE. Digs undertaken by Americans between 1880 and 1948 brought to light two sanctuaries in close proximity: one of Apollo, with the threshold and the altar, the other of Dionysus, whose temple serves as a place for the public display on stone tablets of decrees issued by the Icarians.[8] A marble statue of Dionysus two meters high represented him seated, holding in his hand the cantharus,[9] a wine cup that he never appears to lend to his brother, even in the pictures where Apollo, enveloped in the vine and the bacchanal, appears completely Dionysian.[10] Nearby, by Pythian Apollo's altar, an inscription painted in red letters from around 525 BCE associates Apollo and Dionysus in the dedication of a statue, an *agalma* offered equally to them both.[11] How are they here related? Does not Icarion have special memories of the Dionysus of wine? It is indeed to the village's eponym, Icarius, that Dionysus is supposed to have given vines and wine for the first time, a tragic wine because given without a user's guide. Icarius' guests, thinking themselves poisoned, kill him, which leads to his daughter's suicide and to complete sterility for the land of Icaria: because of the scourge (*loimos*), they rush to Delphi to consult Apollo.[12] The oracle needs no coaxing and immediately offers means to make the scourge cease. It seems that at that very moment Apollo in Delphi is preparing for Dionysus' return, this time through the gate of Eleutheria: this Dionysus will preside at the banquet, at the table of the good king Amphictyon with the city's gods as his symposiasts. We can easily hypothesize that among the gods seated at the table are those enumerated by a Delphic oracle of the fourth century BCE in which the Athenians are ordered not to forget Bacchus, god of ripe fruits (*horaia*), but to form choirs in his honor, to raise kraters, and to illuminate in the streets tile altars of high Zeus (*Hupsistos*), of Heracles, and of Apollo the protector god—*Prostaterios* (he who stands before the door), the *Aguieus* Apollo, god of the highways, of the civilizing roads.[13] The scenario is a familiar one: the misunderstood and forgotten Dionysus is a privileged client of the Apollonian oracle. The god of Delphi, an expert at scourges of all sorts, intervenes for all that must be durably installed, founded, and instituted—for

8 Buck 1892:62–65 (for the threshold of the Pythion), 71–108 (the inscriptions published by Carl Buck). Biers and Boyd 1982 return to the site.
9 Romano 1982:398–409 (pls. 93–95).
10 As Laurens notes in her iconographic analysis written for the Johns Hopkins conference mentioned above.
11 Robinson 1948 (pls. 35–36). Cf. Meyer 1963.
12 Cf. Angiolillo 1981. I have pursued the Dionysus of Ikarion in Detienne 1989a:28–30.
13 Cf. Detienne 1989a:30–33.

instance, the cult of an indispensable god or a new power.[14] When the god of kraters and of the cantharus makes his entrance into the city, Apollo can also meet him "before the doors," and direct his procession amid the burning altars. Back in Icarion, the relation is perfectly clear: the oracle is the domain of Apollo, who knows the paths, brings deliverance from scourges, establishes altars, and founds new cults. To Dionysus belongs wine, its violence as much as its convivial virtue, without any divinatory aspect, and without any "tragedy" as inaugurated by Thespis.

Between Muses and Field Rats

The second configuration appears out at sea, on an island between the water and the sun. In Rhodes, there is neither oracle nor tragedy. Apollo and Dionysus camp side by side in the vineyard, amid the branches and the clusters. Both are charged with a very precise, targeted mission to exterminate the field rats that attack the fruits of the vine. A single epithet defines their function: *Smintheus* (of the field rat). Dionysus is *Smintheus*, as is the Apollo of the *Iliad* when invoked by his humiliated priest; the god *Smintheus* there sends evil, killing dogs, mules, and warriors by the hundreds.[15] But in Rhodes, Apollo of the field rat also asserts himself as god of first-fruits, Apollo of the Thargelia, one of the year's portals that opens the season of fruits. This god is echoed in the Rhodian context by the Dionysus "of fruits" (*Epikarpios*), whose orchard extends beyond the vineyard.[16] The god of the field rat, the Dionysus of Rhodes, presents another two faces: that of the *Bakkheios*, which perfects, possesses, initiates,[17] and that of the *Musagetês*, which conducts and directs the Muses like Apollo, to whom this title belongs more or less officially since Homer and Hesiod. It is interesting to note that in the same place the priest of Dionysus offers sacrifices to the Muses as well as to Mnemosyne, their mother Memory, without forgetting as an object of the same cult Dionysus *Smintheus*, the god of the field rats.[18]

The powers protecting against field rats are so securely in place in Rhodes that they are celebrated in the so-called Sminthia festival with choruses,

---

14 I have written extensively on this in Detienne 1998a, especially in chap. 5, "Fonder-créer une cité: L'oeuvre politique" (105–133).
15 Evidence and analysis in Morelli 1959:41–42 (Dionysus *Smintheus* and the festival of the Sminthia for Apollo and Dionysus), and also 122–25.
16 Ibid., 40.
17 Ibid., 39–41.
18 Ibid., 162–164.

dances, and songs in honor of Apollo and Dionysus.[19] From the organized protection of vines and from the scourge that menaces them, to the conjoined production of rhythms and harmony, the Rhodian configuration suggests a transition managed by the Muses and encountered by Archilochus on Paros, as he interrogates the lyre made by Hermes for Apollo, thereby unmasking the power of music. This transition could bring us back to Delphi and its Muses who are between Dionysus, amusing himself in their company, and the Pythian Apollo, uttering pronouncements more oracular than musical.[20]

The Muses, Apollo, and Dionysus: it is this triad that Plato, without reference to popular beliefs, places in the center of his theory of celebrations and pleasure when he writes the *Laws*.[21] According to the Athenian (who does most of the talking), one day the gods felt compassion for man, ensconced in suffering and misery. More precisely, certain divine powers—Apollo, Dionysus, and the Muses—wishing to grant a reprieve from the ills befalling humanity, gave to it festivals which Plato calls "festival exchanges"; they gave that which is at the heart of *paideia*, of the education of mortals: the experience of rhythm and harmony offered by song and dance—in a word, *khoreia*. The three divinities who invented the festival and the exchange over time divide the educative function among themselves in three successive choirs.[22] The education of children under eighteen years of age belongs to the Muses. Apollo of the Paean guides those who are between eighteen and thirty years of age, the active age of those who constitute the assemblies in Greek cities. Lastly, Dionysus rules over the choir of men from thirty to sixty years of age, those who draw the strength and pleasure of their wisdom from the wine of collective meals and banquets. Dionysus, god of wine amid song and dance, finds himself consecrated as patron of the highest *paideia* in the *Laws*, as if the wisdom of governing well, allopathically produced by catharsis, were more Dionysiac than Apollonian. And yet, at the end of the *Laws*, in the twelfth book,[23] when it comes to defining and enthroning the supreme authority that must guide the new city to its accomplished stature, Plato turns away from Dionysus, preferring Apollo—an Apollo narrowly associated with the Sun, Helios, deemed "the greatest of the gods." There subsists nonetheless something of Dionysus, since the three magistrate-priests designated for the cult of Apollo and the Sun are chosen and elected from the age group

---

19 Ibid., 125.
20 The route would be a little long for the present essay.
21 Plato *Laws* 653a6–654a7.
22 Plato *Laws* 664b–672d.
23 Plato *Laws* 945b–947c. Cf. Boyancé 1972:269–272.

placed under the aegis of Dionysus. Called the Redressers (*Euthunoi*), they will guide the city of Magnesia; the Athenian thinks of these three elders legislating, constantly correcting the direction of the political ship throughout its crossing. Named for life, when they have already reached a venerable age, the Redressers are dedicated to Apollo and to the Sun, as "living tithes and firstfruits" of the human species. After their death, they are heroized, transformed into heroes of the city of Magnesia by their funeral, thus becoming, in the city of the *Laws* founded by Plato, the object of a cult just as political as the one reserved, in most cities newly created since the eighth century BCE, for the colony's founder, promoted at the end of his life to *arkhêgetês*-hero.[24]

To the three-term configuration (Muses, Apollo, and Dionysus) Plato proposes a reconfiguration in which Dionysus, who gives the gift of wine and its cathartic powers to older men,[25] sees himself supervised by a double Apollo, one who directs "political" education along with the Muses, while the second finds himself entrusted with the supreme authority of the city, at the top of the hierarchy of magistrates and priests, itself inspired by the oracle of Delphi and founded by Apollo, guide of the first Magnesians. Indeed, Plato is careful to note that the city of the *Laws*, "founded right from the start, and in a desert landscape" gradually discovers, by following converging clues revealed by its legislators, that it is inhabited by Magnesians—the name of very ancient inhabitants of whom the site has kept such a discreet recollection that the three legislators will need to call upon the god of Delphi to verify this, for he is the ultimate expert on matters of foundation, the divine power deemed the Redresser and Founder of Magnesia in the last chapter of the *Laws*.[26]

An Apollo of the Woods, on the Banks of the Meander

In our provisional experiment a third configuration, neighbor of the preceding one, provides a case of radical exchange between Dionysus and Apollo. A city of Magnesia is once again at hand, but this time it is inscribed in the historians' history and the archeologists' geography. These Magnesians are from the banks of the Meander, in Caria, discovered at the end of the nineteenth century by German investigators who published a rich series of inscriptions, among which was the historical chronicle of the Magnesians from the third

---

24 A reading I have laid out in Detienne 1998a:220–225.

25 On wine and the purification of emotions, cf. the excellent analysis by Belfiore 1986.

26 Plato *Laws* 702d1–2, 704a4–6, 704c6, 848d, 860e, 919d. I have outlined this reading very briefly in Detienne 1990. I have returned to it in a more leisurely fashion in Detienne 1998a:221–223.

century BCE onward.[27] We still do not know whether the author of the *Laws* by using the same name intended to allude to the ancient city of Asia Minor whose founders explicitly pronounced themselves "dedicated to Apollo." However, ancient travelers like to point out the peculiarities of Magnesia on the Meander. In his *Description of Greece*,[28] Pausanias remarks that on the city's territory, in a place called Aulai, there is a rather strange Apollo: a sort of Apollo of the Woods, a cave-dwelling god. The Periegete notes this when he arrives before the so-called Corycian Cave, that deep cavity that Dionysus and the god Pan share high on the mountain overlooking Pythian Apollo's sanctuary. So, outside the city of Magnesia, of which Artemis (*Leukophruene*) is the civic divinity, Apollo lives in a cave. All around, a team of "gardeners" is busy. Their main activity seems to be taking care of the trees of Apollo's garden.[29] However, it sometimes happens that these peaceful horticulturists, having touched the statue of the god in the grotto, act completely differently. They begin to tear up the trees, even the highest ones; they climb up high rocks; they dash through the narrowest paths carrying the uprooted trunks. Apollo's gardeners act as if possessed: filled with Apollo's strength (*iskhus*),[30] they begin the mountain race that Euripides calls *oribasia* and that he stages in the *Bacchae*. There the women of Thebes, possessed by Dionysus, leap about the forest, uproot trees, and go so far as to rip into pieces randomly encountered cattle and wild beasts. But whereas the Bacchae abandon the houses and streets of the city, those maddened by Apollo rush toward the city of Magnesia. Their Dionysiac craze leads them to the heart of the city, to the agora where, surprisingly enough, the god Dionysus is waiting for them—a serene, smiling Dionysus, seated on the "box," the *kiste* of mysteries. Various

27 The record on Apollo and Dionysus in Magnesia on the Meander was the subject of an initial essay of mine published under the rather general title, "Apollo und Dionysos in der griechischen Religion" (1986). A second version would not be unwelcome. Here I shall confine myself to a certain number of traits and minimal references.

28 Pausanius 10.32.6 Rocha-Pereira (Leipzig, 1981), who has included the correction proposed by Wilamowitz. The two most important studies are Robert 1977:77–88 and 1978:538–543, who reports the realia, lays out the facts, and shows no curiosity about the question of polytheism (i.e. the system of relations between Apollo and Dionysus at Magnesia on the Meander and in a series of sites). *Ne sutor ultra crepidam*—but what a shoemaker!

29 It is worth recalling that the "Gardeners of Apollo" are known through an epigraphic document, a "letter of Darius" (522–486 BCE), published in the collection of Meiggs and Lewis 1975:20–22, no. 12. The authenticity of the letter has recently been defended by the excellent arguments of Boffo 1978.

30 Which it would be appropriale to analyze with regard to the *dunamis* of Dionysus and the condition of the *automaton*; cf. "The Heart of Dionysos Bared," the final chapter of Detienne 1989a:57–64.

coins represent different phases of the scenario. We know the story of this "city-center" Dionysus thanks to local chronicles engraved on stone and published by Otto Kern.[31] One day a very violent wind rends the plane tree of the main square. Inside the tree there appears an effigy of Dionysus. The oracle is consulted, that of Delphi of course, because Apollo is the founder of the city of Magnesia, the *arkhêgetês* who rules in Magnesia on Meander as the high god along with Artemis *Leukophruene*, the civic goddess. Apollo's oracle reminds the Magnesians, "they who had been dedicated to the Pythian," that in building their city they forgot a god who "was already there," on the site marked by an ancient oracle. This god, Dionysus lodged in the plane tree, must immediately be recognized, given a temple, offered *thiasoi*; his mysteries must be installed under the direction of the maenads; these must be taken for healing immediately to Thebes, the mother city of Dionysus that once experienced ignorance of this great god.

This time the cave-dwelling Apollo of Magnesia borrows from Dionysus his apparently most specific trait: *mania*, the power that flings one outside of oneself and drags one far away from familiar places, be it wild nature or an invaded city. If delirium, furious folly, and enthusiasm are no strangers to Apollo, those whom he seizes, whether women or men, most often act as diviners and prophets. Those whom Apollo maddens do not form *thiasoi*; they are not possessed as a group and then released by him, as are Dionysus' people, the *Bakkhoi*. Conversely, the maenads, those maddened by Dionysus, practice neither prophecy nor divination, nor does anyone possessed by him. The force that Apollo of the woods and the cave bestows upon his faithful gardeners of Magnesia shows itself to be at the service of a Dionysus who is of the tree, indeed, but also of the public square, awaiting the arrival of these Magnesians "dedicated to Apollo" and walking the paths of the Pythian's words. Several Dionysuses answer to Apollo's complexity in this configuration on the Meander: the Dionysus of mysteries, at the heart of the initiation taken on by the three *thiasoi* of Theban origin—the domain of "telestic" as Greeks call it, which Dionysus shares with other gods but seemingly not with Apollo—is added onto the "dendrite" (under-the-tree's-bark) power, and to the god publicly recognized by Delphi.

---

31 Without reviewing the record, let us recall at least the document (no. 17) published in Kern 1900.

Wine as Catalyst

It is not enough to note that the Magnesians of Caria came from Delphi, according to their written traditions, only to decide immediately to return toward Parnassus. The three preceding configurations are deployed to offer the experimentalist the opportunity of a series of catalysts in order to practice a differential microanalysis of a fragment of polytheism. Wine, like a red cord running between Icarion and Rhodes, presents a first catalyst from which Apollo, first of all, cannot hide, ever since we caught him in the company of Dionysus protecting the vineyard against a scourge. Wine is the liquid with which Dionysus is so completely associated that he is sometimes identified with it: "We pour him as a libation to the gods, he, a god himself."[32] This transubstantiation does not threaten Apollo at all, no more than most of the other divine powers. What does this drink, so rich in *dunamis*, represent for a god such as Apollo? What of Apollo, if the force of wine is like lightning, if when one absorbs it nearly pure the trance courses through one's veins, if "it is *bakkhie* itself," as Archilochus cries out from Paros (frag. 194 W)? For Apollo too is the god of possession, an expert in *mania*, whose diviner in the *Odyssey* notably behaves as if hallucinating; Theoclymenus prophecies red death at the banquet when he sees black blood running from the suitors' jaws while they devour, as they do every day, the chunks of meat for their evening meal. Apollo, so present in sacrificial ceremonies, is no stranger to wine. For instance at Naucratis, a Greek city founded around 650 in Egyptian territory, one of whose numerous temples is a sanctuary dedicated to Hestia, called *Prutanis*,[33] thus designating it as the place for a group aware of its autonomy to exercise sovereignty. On her festival day, which appears to be the birthdate of the city, Hestia receives Dionysus' priest and Apollo's priest at the same time. On that day, they both get a double serving of wine. What is this Apollo who is invited into Hestia's house, he who was an unhappy suitor of hers, just like Poseidon? He is firstly the Pythian, the god of Delphi, more or less Founder, even if we do not know him clothed as *Arkhêgetês*. Next, he is the Apollo of the Banquet (*Kômaios*), the god of *kômos*, of the banquet of serious drinking. In addition, we know that on the day of Hestia's festival, the flute players were invited into the Prytaneion, a space from which women are carefully excluded on other days.

---

32 Euripides *Bacchae* 248. It would be quite useful to consider the signification of wine and its place in sacrificial ritual and thereby return to the question of the *nephalia* (wineless rites).

33 Cf. Detienne 1985a:59–78, taken up again in 1989b:85–98, esp. 96–98. The important text is that of Hermeias *On the Gryneian Apollo*—Athenaeus 4.149d = F 112 Tresp.

Nothing allows us to think that Apollo's priest would leave immediately after having taken his double ration of wine. We have therefore a slightly tottering Apollo, at least in the representation of his priest; this is easily supported first of all with a reminder that he takes pleasure in inebriating the Erinyes (Aesch. *Eumenides* 727–728), those old divinities of spilt blood who complained of the young god's insolence when he slyly served them an unknown beverage, which they took for their usual potion of honey cut with water and lapped up. If we are to believe the pictures on Attic vases, Apollo is quite at ease amid the satyrs and maenads while wine flows abundantly. However, as A.-F. Laurens notes,[34] Apollo apparently never holds the cantharus (drinking cup), which Dionysus jealously keeps to himself. Reciprocally, in the same imagery, Apollo's lyre never gets into Dionysus' hands though he is passionate about music and such a willing lyre player. In the musical area where they meet between Muses and maenads, instruments are also excellent catalysts defining segments of the boundaries between Dionysus and Apollo.

On the Medical Vocation

Protecting vines against scourges that menace them does not imply that Apollo is their inventor, or that he grants this gift to humanity. Presiding at the banquet and enjoying the company of the maenads does not make Apollo a god of the cantharus or of flowing wine barrels. He is, however, linked to another aspect of wine: its medicinal qualities.[35] Apollo and Dionysus are both well-known doctors. Wine has long possessed therapeutic virtues abundantly described from Hippocrates to Galen. God of wine, Dionysus has a medical vocation: he is called Doctor (*Iatros*). This becomes even more comprehensible when we adjust the lens, focusing on the medical aspect of a Dionysus of wine. Let us consult the fourth-century doctors. Mnesitheus, for example, an excellent dietician and author of a "Letter on Drinking Much," specifies that the Pythian priestess had advised some not to call Dionysus Doctor (*Iatros*), but rather Dispenser of Health (*Hugiatês*).[36] This distinction reveals the distance from Apollo, who is also a doctor (*iatros*), but who is not immediately drawn toward the field of health or diet. The health, not of the individual body but of the political body of the whole city, is the domain of Apollo the Doctor. It is to Delphi, to Apollo's oracle, that people flock to ask

---

34 In the same presentation to the Johns Hopkins conference (see notes above).
35 A body of evidence established by Jouanna 1996.
36 Mnesitheus frags. 41 and 42 Bertier; cf. Detienne 1989a:38–39.

what is to be done when a scourge crops up, when the city is struck by disease (*nosos*), be it evil births, monsters vomited forth by the earth, civil war, or horrible dissension between citizens. Most often the Pythian priestess invites the supplicant to view the scourge or the collective illness as the symptom of an impurity or an ancient mistake. This political practice of medicine is situated at the intersection of the virtues of the founder god and the protector god, of the *Arkhêgetês* Apollo, and of the *Prostaterios* Apollo.[37] The Doctor Apollo cannot be equated with Dionysus of good wine. Analysis would profit from questioning the relations between Doctor Apollo and his son Asclepius and from asking what form of health *Hugeia* Athena, who is also "a dispenser of health" allows us to distinguish; and why Poseidon appears as a doctor at Tenos while elsewhere it is Artemis. Religious representations of the medical field would benefit from this as much as would the complexity of each divine power tested under these circumstances.

A scourge (*loimos*) or an illness (*nosos*), with the collective dimension of both, also offers an excellent catalyst to distinguish Apollo from Dionysus from the point of view of impurity and purification as well as divination, much in demand in the case of epidemics, and of which, let us be reminded, both seem to be guarantors at Delphi. An epidemic, in the nonmedical Greek sense of an ill befalling a large number of people, is not Apollo's exclusive domain. When all the women of the land suddenly become wild and throw themselves into a frenzied race, when all the males of a region are stricken with satyriasis and find themselves in a painful state of erection without being able to end it, it is Dionysus who is showing himself. And what does one do in this case? The same thing as in the preceding case: the oracle at Delphi is again consulted. It might seem that Dionysus could seize this occasion to render an oracle in the sanctuary he is said to share with his brother. Yet the god of wine, of folly, or of permanent erections never speaks out at Delphi to say what must be done. If there is a scourge, an epidemic, or a collective ill, it is Apollo's affair. From the *Iliad* to the end of antiquity the scourge as a symptom belongs to the Pythian's domain. When it is time to say that an epidemic of folly was provoked by the anger of an ignored god and that it is urgent to build him a temple, Dionysus again allows Apollo to act. Let us note in passing that in the sanctuary, Dionysus makes his appearance when his brother leaves the oracle. He is only there in passing. He is hibernating, such that a squadron of Bubbling Women, the Thyiades, is apparently specifically

---

37 Apollo the doctor and the seer who responds to plagues that strike the city is outlined in Detienne 1998a.

charged with waking him, pulling him from his winter sleep. But whether Dionysus is awake or asleep, not a single oracular word springs from his mouth, at least at Delphi. Let us briefly say before coming back to it more at length elsewhere that Dionysus has nothing to do with all that is lastingly set up, at once founded and created by the oracular words and by the founding god of all that must be founded. Perhaps there is here a fairly clear dividing line between Apollo and Dionysus in general.

Let us once again forget Delphi in order to suggest another discontinuity that brings us back, through folly, to impurity and to the purification—more precisely, the folly that is *mania*, which both gods experience personally, in their individual histories. Because he is Semele's son, the child Dionysus is a victim of Hera's anger. She infects him with folly, a *mania* of which Dionysus will be cured and purified only when Rhea, wife of Cronus, initiates him to his own Bacchic mysteries by giving him the Bacchant costume, the vestment-mask which Dionysus in turn has his initiates put on, who thus become "Bacchants" in his image.[38] Much like a scourge, folly is perceived as an illness, and this illness is marked by impurity. The impurity of the scourge that is folly, either murderous or possessed, demands purification that delivers and frees from the impure.

Parallel to Dionysus, Apollo existentially knows demons and tastes furious folly in his own way. This happens at Sicyon, the ancient Mekone, where Hesiod situates the division between men and gods. Apollo spilled the Python serpent's blood and the powers of murder take hold of him, drive him to madness, push him to flee to the heart of Crete to obtain the help of an incomparable purifier, Carmanor. This impure god was cured of his folly and entertains close relations with a series of murderers come to the oracle at Delphi; he will entrust them with the founding of new cities under the patronage of *Arkhêgetês* Apollo. They are thus "dedicated" to this Apollo while they are also purified of their impurity and of their folly.[39]

The "impurity-purification" catalyst is particularly interesting when it demonstrates the different modes of action of Dionysus and Apollo. The furious Dionysus who puts on the mask of delivery and purification chooses the road of initiation, whether it is for mortals to be introduced to the plea- sure of wine, or to be led to recognize the power of an unrecognized god, or suddenly to see the god face-to-face by becoming his initiate, by having

---

38 Following the account of the *Bibliotheca* of Apollodorus (3.5.1), the importance of which for understanding the *mania* of Dionysus has not diminished, in my opinion; see Detienne 1989a:21–22.

39 The major evidence is Pausanius 2.7.7–9. One suspects that the "impure" god, the Apollo of Murderers, plays a greater role than necessary in the work cited.

access to his mysteries. But the Handsome Homicide of Delphi, to whom one comes for advice on deliverance from a scourge or the purification of an ancient fault, invites the impure to give himself a regenerated space, to go away toward the unknown, to cut out a new territory and become a Founder, completely separated from his past, two orientations that seem radically different and that show two lines or two activities that are not shared or traded between Dionysus and Apollo. As for the pleasure of founding and being *arkhêgetês*, Dionysus does not really seem to appreciate it.

Other analyses open out from these. Where there is *mania*, furious folly, several gods are immediately available: Ares, the furious lunatic; Lyssa, Rage; Artemis; the Nymphs; as well as Hera, who scrambles the mind of more than one mortal. If we wish to start from murder in relation to various gods, we must first confront the Zeus of Murderers,[40] who simultaneously pursues them and insures their ritual purification, with his son Apollo, impure and murderous god, rising up against his father's authority, with Dionysus in mind, who does not advertise himself as a murderer but contents himself with inciting certain of his possessed to slit the throats of their own children or tear them up. Or, even though it may require a larger context, the experimentalist will learn from a comparison of the respective choices of the Pythagoreans, in all appearance exclusive devotees of Apollo, and of Orpheus' disciples, so attentive to Dionysus, or at least to certain aspects of this god. This route proposes from the onset a series of catalysts: music, its modes, its instruments; sacrifice, its refusal, its modalities in relation to war, murder, and "vegetarianism"; political foundation and reform; asceticism and models of initiation or of lifestyle. So we collect an ensemble of manipulations and experimental approaches that allow the progressive discovery of the complex texture of a polytheistic system where each god is first of all *in the plural.*

---

40 The so-called sacred law of Selinous invites one to examine more closely the Zeus of Murderers and Suppliants.

PART III

"Politics" Doesn't Fall from the Sky

1

Doing Comparative Anthropology in the Field of Politics*

HERE IS A LONG HISTORY behind the Greeks and us. Clearly, the Greeks are not a tribe or even an ethnic group like others. At the heart of what historians complacently call "the history of the West," the Greeks represent a real stake, in the sense of what may be either won or lost in an enterprise.

I am happy that André Breton has reminded us that in the past, in both the ancient and the modern world, the Greeks and Romans "have always been our occupiers" and will continue to be in the future. It is important to realize that, among the ancient societies, it was the Greeks—not the Egyptians or the Sumerians—who spoke and wrote the most, with words and categories that we ourselves have never ceased to use, often without even thinking about it. One of the most blindingly obvious examples, alongside that of "mythology," is, both in the ancient and now in the modern world, in the domain of what is known as "politics."

It is widely believed in the United States of Europe and of America that democracy fell from the skies once and for all, to land in Greece and even in one particular city there, Pericles' Athens. Since the eighteenth century, the interpretation of other, more revolutionary beginnings has repeatedly proceeded by way of dialogue with that city. In the memories of Europeans, inaugurations of democracy hold an important place. The Italians like to look back to the communal movement of the twelfth and thirteenth centuries; the English, the first to dare to behead a king, are happy to contemplate their House of Commons, while the French, with good reason, set a high value on the radical break constituted by 1789. All these national traditions are respected, if not respectable. They belong to the Europe that is in the making; and the historians of its various nations have certainly not failed to show that they

* Originally published in *Arion* 13.3 (Winter 2006) 67–85.

deserve respect, even as they carefully avoid comparisons which, as they see it, are not necessary, given the differences in chronology. Besides, comparisons might offend national memories over which, above all in Europe, the writers of History naturally take it upon themselves to mount vigilant guard.

Multiple Beginnings

As a result, more often than not, historians of politics, closely followed by political theorists, limit comparisons between ancient and modern democracies to value judgments, the most popular of which leads one to wonder whether the Athenians did *really* experience democracy. For it is Athens, preferably the Athens of Thucydides, that seems, over two centuries, to have become the sole example worthy to enter into dialogue with the "real" democracies that have colonized both sides of the Atlantic, God be praised! As everyone knows or can easily find out, in the space of two centuries, between the eleventh and the thirteenth, the beginnings of the communal movement in Italy mobilized dozens of towns; and in ancient Greece, there were several hundreds of small human communities experimenting over more than three hundred years with a would-be egalitarian form of politics. In Tuscany and Venetia, even the smallest communes engaged in an adventure that involved making choices that would carry them into a history of their own. And likewise, from the eighth century BCE on (just yesterday!), each of those tiny cities in Sicily or along the shores of the Black Sea set about inventing their own ways of deliberating and deciding on "common affairs." The little town of Draco and then of Solon—I mean that village, Athens, of modest beginnings—represented but one type of city among dozens of others, all enjoying the same freedom of creating their own completely new practices of communal living.

Comparison, but not of a parochial kind, is an immediately effective way of escaping from the claustrophobic sense of being trapped between an endless "Greek miracle" and an incurably obese "Western civilization." For thirty years now, the field of comparison has been expanding to include other societies and new continents.[1] For example, historians of Ukraine and the Russian world have rediscovered the surprisingly "democratic" manners of the Cossacks of the fifteenth to seventeenth centuries.[2] Meanwhile, anthropologists who went to southern Ethiopia to investigate kinship systems

---

1 I have already argued and worked to this end in Detienne 2000b:105–127; and in "Des pratiques d'assemblée aux formes du politique" (2003b:13–30), and "Retour sur comparer et arrêt sur comparables" (2003b:415–418).

2 See the works of Iaroslav Lebedynsky, cited in Lebedynsky 2003.

there have been bringing back in their nets a whole haul of autochthonous assembly practices that mark out "places for politics," as Marc Abélès, one of the discoverers, has called them.[3]

Even without waiting for the discoveries of other observers of human beings—who tend today to be very anxious not to be accused of ethnographic harassment—it seems fair enough to note that such "places for politics" have been invented many times over in societies widely separated from one another by both time and space. The Ochollo people of the Gamo mountains, who have been living in southern Ethiopia since the nineteenth century, do not, so far, appear to have consulted the communal archives of Siena or Arezzo; nor did the fifteenth-century Cossacks of Zaporizhia necessarily discover from the *Iliad*, let alone from the site of Megara Hyblaea in Sicily, the principle of an agora and a circular community assembly—a principle that dates from, at the very least, the eighth century BCE. As for the French members of the Constituent Assembly of 1789, although they were relatively well informed about the English system that had been in place for several centuries, they seem to have had to, and to have wished to, invent everything themselves from scratch, on the more or less tabula rasa left by what would soon be called the ancien régime. From historians who are liberated enough not to bother about the constraints imposed by the order that governs them, anthropologists have learned that certain cultures in both Africa and the Slavic world have, both in the past and in contemporary times, set in place forms of "democracy" in assemblies convened to debate the group's "common affairs." It is time to recognize that there has been no more an Ochollo miracle than there was a Greek or a Cossack one.

Places for Politics

Politics and Places for Politics: it is commonly believed not only that politics or Politics (with a capital *P*) one fine day fell from the heavens, landing in "classical" Athens in the miraculous and authenticated form of Democracy (with a capital *D*), but also that a divinely linear history has led us by the hand from the American Revolution, passing by way of the "French Revolution," all the way to our own Western societies that are so blithely convinced that their mission is to convert all peoples to the true religion of democracy.

---

3 In this comparative branch of study, Marc Abélès has played an important role: first, with his book *Le lieu du politique* (Abélès 1983), then with his "Revenir chez les Ochollo" (Abélès 2003).

I must emphasize that the comparative approach that I have chosen is the work of a group consisting of both historians and anthropologists; it must be experimental, and its aim is to be constructive: "comparabilities" have to be constructed in an experimental fashion.

It is, I think, indispensable to explain clearly what kinds of operations this type of comparative method involves, in order to show how progress, carefully thought through, can be made.

First of all, I tried to move on from the Greek city, leaving other enthusiastic scholars to determine the date of birth of "Politics," not to mention find all the fashionable expressions in which the subject is decked in the smartest Houses of High Fashion in Munich, the Latin quarter of Paris, and Cambridge.

Next, it seemed to me healthy to wipe the slate clean and reject all ready-made definitions of "Politics." Wipe the slate clean . . . but how clean? Leaving only the practices of assembly; in particular, practices observed in situations where such an institution is being initiated so that, with any luck, those practices take simple forms. What I am talking about are practices of assembly or, more precisely, practices associated with a will to gather together, *a will to assemble.* That is the first point. But assemble in order to do what? To *discuss common affairs.* That is the second point, but it is not an innocent one, for I have found it necessary to make a very specific choice. This is not a matter of gathering together for a fishing expedition or in order to barter feathers against claws. I realize how very porous and insecure the apparently firmest frontiers can turn out to be; but a definition such as "procedures involving words used to express an idea of that which is common" can perhaps delimit a provisional context for this "will to assemble together"—a context within which something like politics or even a "place for politics" may be constructed. As can be seen, this kind of comparative study is "experimental."

I think that one advantage of this deliberate choice of the concept of "a will to assemble together in order to discuss common affairs" is that it provides an initial working category that is flexible yet not too fluid. This is not a general paradigm such as, for example, the civic "humanism" or *vivere civile* that John Pocock proposes, a setup with a prince as political agent, surrounded by his homegrown Florentine associates: the citizen, the orator, and the inspired legislator. That concept may, to be sure, serve as a way to penetrate the post-sixteenth-century Anglo-Saxon world, but it is as unexportable as the category of "empire." The "will to assemble together" as described above is neither a category that is too local nor a notion that is too general, of the "catchall" type.

The category selected for an inquiry published in 2000 thus led very directly into a series of questions relating to concrete practices.[4] Who sets in train the process of assembling together? Is it just any member of the group? Or is it an elder, a man with authority, an elected leader? Or an individual endowed with religious powers? Where is the assembly held? In a place that changes from one assembly to the next? Or in a place that is marked out, a fixed venue specially arranged or even architecturally designed for the purpose? Are rituals associated with this place? Discreet rituals? Solemn ones? Who opens such an assembly and who brings it to a close? Who presides over it, and how? Is it preceded by a smaller council meeting, or not? What type of council? Is there some kind of agenda? How does one gain the right to speak? By making some gesture? What gesture? If there is an argument, what form does it take? Does it involve "contradiction" or not? What about the assembly calendar? Is the assembly held at regular intervals? Is this will to assemble urgent or calm? Does the assembly come to a final decision, and if so, how? By acclamation? By a show of hands? By secret voting? By a majority vote? What is the status of the minority? Does the assembly need a quorum in order to operate? What proportion of the total membership of the assembly or the community does the quorum involve?

As cooperation between ethnologists and historians progresses, the more questions become precise and the more differences proliferate, much to the benefit of the experiment. As can be seen, the important thing is to encourage reflection on the complexity of the structure of something that could be called "politics."

The other advantage of the approach through study of "the will to assemble together" is that it allows one easily to acquire a perspective on a whole series of societies as diverse and as far-flung from one another as the Italian communes of the European Middle Ages; the Buddhist monasteries of Japan; the members of the French Constituent Assembly; the Cossacks who lived at the time of Macchiavelli's *Prince;* the Ochollo people in today's Ethiopia; the Circassians of the last century; the Senoufo of the Ivory Coast; the sleek, plump, secular canons of the medieval West; and the tiny cities of Magna Graecia and Sicily—in short, a whole score of cultures mobilized in the course of the first stage of a collaborative investigation: twenty societies studied not in general, but as microconfigurations analyzed by researchers working from within, many of them for as long as twenty years.

---

4 Detienne 2003b, an inquiry that I initiated in 1992, in Marseilles, where I encountered the first difficulties (417–418) and concluded in its "colloquial" phase in Paris, at the Fondation des Sciences politiques (in 2000).

Comparing Beginnings

Start with simple forms, observe the practices of beginnings, work on micro-configurations, for they are easier to compare, as "comparables," than complex or semicomplex states stiffly hemmed in by their macroconfigurations. To be sure, beginnings take multiple forms and are widely diverse. They come about sometimes in a virtually empty space, on a tabula rasa or a leveled foundation flush with the ground; sometimes in highly sophisticated contexts. The birth pangs of what we might call a "place for politics" are never the same from one society to another. The first Cossacks, self-proclaimed free men, had only the steppe with its icy silence. For all those Lilliputian cities traced out in the sand of Magna Graecia, there was, to begin with, virgin land that at first sight seemed unoccupied. For the revolutionary Pisans of the 1080 Marine Commune, there were, on the contrary, already the town, its nobles, the imperial authorities and, closer to home, the Church authorities. Facing the members of the French Constituent Assembly, as they tried to convert their semicircle into a full circle, there was what would soon be called the ancien régime, the king and a hierarchical society of orders and privileges to fall upon and dismantle with hammer blows.

Let us keep an eye on those members of the Constituent Assembly, those mutants of 1789, for that was a fascinating beginning that is easy to observe. From the springboard of its formidable "will to assemble together" in order to discuss the affairs of one and all (the expression was certainly spot on), it proceeded passionately to invent a series of assembly practices and to dream up a new kind of space for permanent deliberations between "the nation's representatives," each of whom, in principle, held an equal right to speak on everything that concerned the welfare of the people—the people who were soon to be consecrated as sovereign. Along with a multitude of new practices, there emerged ideas expressed by a number of different voices on the subject of a new kind of place for politics that recognized no precedents. The virtue of such beginnings is that they reveal how configurations take shape and what elements combine to produce the idea of a community, ways of organizing a kind of group-sovereignty, of structuring a public space and exploring a type of citizenship.

Possible Comparabilities

Far-flung comparison constitutes an intellectual game that affords one the pleasure of collaborative, unhurried experimentation. To provide you with a glimpse of what it involves, let me convey a bird's eye view of some of the factors that it has proved possible to compare within the vast domain of "who wishes to speak?" (the title that we chose for our comparative inquiry, because it seemed to echo the formulaic demand of a herald opening an assembly in a Greek city).

The simplest way to do this is to put together a collection of notions that seem to operate as good litmus tests in the field of "the will to assemble together" for clearly defined purposes. Let us focus on three such notions: the notion of "public matters" or common affairs; the notion of "citizenship" (in quotation marks); and finally the pair constituted by "sameness-equality."

Public Matters

If one selects for special study the theme of the concrete ways of assembling together, one has a chance to observe how the representation of communal affairs may be affected by the practices that stem from a local will to assemble together. A will: let us pause to consider what this implies. Sometimes people flock together; sometimes they are assembled. A king or a chieftain can order people to assemble. They flock together when something unexpected happens, when there is an accident, when something surprises the passers-by. They are told to keep moving, there is nothing to see. But the will to assemble together for precise purposes is always the work of a minority, an active minority. What motivates such a minority? Without necessarily expecting a satisfactory explanation, let us rephrase that question in terms of certain types of people who carry more influence than others.

I chose the formula of a herald of antiquity not because it is Greek (for no one could accuse me of Hellenomania), but because it introduces a "will" without which this particular kind of politics—one kind among many others— oriented toward the debate of public affairs, could neither be instituted nor expand and develop. To have a place reserved for the discussion of affairs that are *common* to individuals who are naturally different and spontaneously unequal may seem a strange idea. "The will to assemble together" appears to impose itself progressively through the adoption of practices and a kind of setting that reveal to the group something like the beginnings of sovereignty,

sovereignty for the group over itself. For the people engaged in this work—work that is quite taxing—to discuss affairs said to concern all, to speak of what is felt and recognized to be most essential to the group, involves their finding new representations, which they do by all adopting particular practices and making use of convergent symbolisms.

A place for politics or a place of equality in the making may seem pretty unremarkable. Let us pick out a few groups at random: secular canons were expected to discuss common affairs together three times a week. They elaborated a fair system of remuneration to compensate for the considerable inequalities between them. But the *universitas*, the name for "whatever was common" to these secular clergy, was strengthened by the choice of a central meeting place such as the bell-tower or a particular hall that could be used by the citizens and townsfolk. The *universitas* of the canons included a coffer for the storage of archives and a seal that conferred a measure of authority. The Cossacks, whether from Zaporozhye or from the area of the Don, certainly did not meet two or three times a week, but they observed a far stricter equality that initially covered every domain of activity: warfare, hunting, fishing, and the cultivation of the land. The "community" (*tovaristvo*, in Ukrainian) was present here. It existed not only when all the Cossacks formed a circle several ranks deep in the main square, but also when the mace of the military leader, the seal of the judges, and the great silver inkwell of the secretary were deposited at the center of the assembly. To represent and symbolize "that which is common," the earliest Greek cities had the idea, not of money or a sacrificial altar, but of a public hearth in the guise of Hestia, a common hearth corresponding to the Romans' Vesta. This embodied the idea of a united city in the place where the magistrates in charge of common affairs congregated every day. In medieval Japan, the meetings of Buddhist monks took a different form. The assembly was preceded by an oath of union and harmony. Each man present was in duty bound to tell the whole community all that concerned "each and every one of them," and an assembly that regarded itself as unanimous considered that its decisions and judgments were passed with the gods as witnesses.

Citizenships in the Making

A second notion that may also prove to be of practical use is that of "citizenship"—an excellent litmus test in the field of political potentials. For example, all you need to do is determine what are the qualities that are desirable or required for anyone who insists on assembling to speak exclusively of common affairs. Within the circle where the question "Who wishes to speak?" is asked, who are these first orators? What must they be? What must they have? How do they claim to be qualified? For example, the "equal rights" of citizens decreed by the French Revolution had no meaning outside the philosophical context of the eighteenth century. But what was the concrete meaning of "the right to equality" when the Declaration of Human Rights was proclaimed and published, against the background of the dissolution of a regime of orders with hierarchical privileges? The appearance of twenty million citizens overnight did not mean that there arose from the earth active citizens, committed at every national level to participation in public affairs. In 1789, to possess a theoretical right to equality it was enough to have been "born in France," but for the militants of primary or sectional assemblies, everything still remained to be organized. Now let us consider the groups of Greeks, two hundred or five hundred strong, such as those who, in the eighth and seventh centuries BCE, were to establish themselves on the seashores somewhere between Sicily and the Black Sea. Their potential "citizenship" began with the tracing of a circle, called an *agora* (or assembly), or possibly with a drawing of lots for plots of land, either before their departure or aboard the ship itself. Each man, with his own set of weapons, seems already to have possessed an equal right to take part in debates and in sacrifices of foodstuffs made by the group as a whole. To participate and take part with an equal share in anything that belonged to whatever was "in common" or concerned the city (*polis*) constituted the pulsing heart of this early type of citizenship centered on a fixed space reserved for assemblies, public debates, battles of words concerning the common affairs of an as yet barely established group. It is within these new places of equality and possibly "of politics" that we can best observe the elements that combine to produce "citizenship" centered on "common affairs." It was not enough to be a local and to live on one's own plot of land. An individual also had to be part of the circle formed by the deliberative assembly and to take a hand in the dispensing of justice within another circle or a circle within a circle. How did "citizens" wish to act as a group, and to what extent was it possible for them to do so? The nations of the past and their successive experiments in this domain are very useful for distinguishing different types of citizenship and the criteria that make it possible to distinguish "citizens" from foreigners passing through or in residence among them, and to establish a scale of gradations between those whose arrival could be accepted and those who could, to varying degrees, be integrated and "naturalized." For instance, should they or should they not be allowed access to public offices, to the highest posts as magistrates or to other functions essential to the city or group? It has been noticed that, sooner or later, the assembly—the *universitas* or Community—would come to expect active citizens to manifest certain qualities before it ruled that they clearly did possess specific capabilities of a kind to guide the *respublica* or its equivalent in a decisive fashion.

Those Who Are All the Same and Equal

A third point of entry or notion on which reflection proves rewarding is "sameness-equality." One hypothesis is that "a will to assemble together in order to deliberate on common affairs" presupposes that everyone recognizes all the others in this circle to be the same and somehow equal. The first analogy that springs to mind does not create a sameness great enough to envisage the possibility of "a common interest." Rousseau thought that the citizenship of the ancients was inspired by a common sensitivity born of the familiarity and compassion that existed among members of a very small community. He thought that, in those times, a General Will sprang up and flowed spontaneously. But the existence of similar sentiments and opinions is surely not the only conceivable basis for a community. The Cossacks shared a common desire to be "free men" in the midst of princes and serfs, and all called one another "brothers." Their common father was a leader whom they chose for themselves every year at the assembly of all the "brothers" who, through the practices of equality that they observed, were all "the same" and "equal." At the start, the Cossacks were all "free men," just as the participants in the first commune of eleventh-century Pisa were, for the most part, "free" seamen who all shared the same struggle at sea. In other groups, all the members were Buddhist monks or secular canons.

In some societies, that sameness and equality was proclaimed explicitly, once a certain level of "the will to assemble" was reached. For example, in ancient Greece, in the tiny cities of the archaic period, each man held *equal rights* and *shared equally* in the privileges of "citizenship." Such sameness presupposes that the distinctive features that, at a different level, distinguished men of different social status and with varying links of kinship would be set aside. Mutual recognition of forms of sameness may contribute to the creation of the idea of a community or city; and practices of equality, for their part, have a constituent force. First there is an arithmetical equality in the distribution of land, of booty, or of food, all of which is allocated in equal portions by the drawing of lots. Geometric equality soon follows, in a variety of formulations. Equality is something that needs to be made explicit, discussed in public, and, in the usual way of things, fought for at every stage and at every assembly level.

One example, a concrete case, will show how practices of "assembling together" can produce and fashion something like "Politics." On a particular "campus," why not decide to "invent a *universitas*" in a very empirical fashion?[5] Between the eleventh and twelfth centuries, Italian communes sprouted like mushrooms after the rain, each one as a local experiment within a new public space. In general, the first thing that happened was that a collective group or *universitas* took shape, claiming an autonomy that aimed for self-government and the institution of an authority that was both secular and temporal. For this communal movement surfaced deep in the midst of a society subject to the omnipresent authority of the Christian Church and also to that of the Germanic Holy Roman Empire. Gatherings before cathedrals when courts of justice were set up cannot be confused with the deliberate, planned assembly of seamen-citizens that took place in Pisa in 1080. This decreed itself to be a *communitas* and assumed the right to organize and finance armed expeditions of the fleet. Elsewhere too, the conquest of a civil space proceeded step by step, involving a whole series of microscopic regulatory measures; the alignment of houses, the positioning of streets, the management of town gates, and the design of public places.

Consuls, assemblies, and councils continued to be features characteristic of the history of communal practices. (It is perhaps worth noting, in passing, that many such communes are still awaiting a historian.) One primary aspect of this world of communes is the role played by notaries and jurists. Dispensing justice and declaring the rights of citizens are activities that go hand in hand with the work of notaries who consign the debates to written records, thereby formulating practices many of which are without precedent. Another feature that played an important role in the creation of communal assemblies was the taking of an oath, an oath of solidarity and loyalty to the collective decisions that committed the community to action. In some cases such an oath would be individual, in others collective. It indicated that the will to assemble counted for more than mere traditional gatherings. What forms of citizenship do we find developing in the emerging "city-republics"? What was the basis of the sameness of those who agreed to decide together on affairs that affected the *communitas* as a whole? An assembly, which might be called a "parliament," in many cases seems to have consisted of a *populus*, in other words all those capable of bearing arms on both land and sea, who

5 See Delumeau 2003, Rosetti 2003, and Redon 2003.

must have possessed sufficient means to pay for arms and, in some cases, a horse. Here and there, we find instances of a *populus* that splits away from the *milites* who fight on horseback while the rest continue to do so on foot. Councils restricted to between three and five hundred members set about preparing the agenda and discussing the major issues before submitting them to a general assembly that might be composed of between five and six thousand members. Some modes of election involved the drawing of lots, others did not. There were rules relating to majority votes, the definition of a quorum, and the roles of experts and social leaders. All such procedures varied from one commune to another and produced types of politics that inevitably varied from one place to another.

Another Example of Very Concrete Practices: The House of Commons and the Members of the French Constituent Assembly

The scene changes. In France, the theater of representation is the Constituent Assembly; in England, the House of Commons. There is also a temporal disparity here. When the French Revolution of 1789 began, English political customs had long been developing. In the fourteenth and fifteenth centuries, the London Parliament had been extremely active. The French Constituent Assembly inaugurated a new space for speech. The sovereignty of the People required a new public space: there were disputes over the advantages of a circle and those of a semicircle. In 1792, new practices were introduced, at the instigation of both Marseilles and Paris. It was no longer just a matter of every individual's right to assemble; now every citizen was claiming the right "to make the law speak." It was time to move beyond the restricted circle of the Assembly and representatives. Room had to be made for the missionaries of patriotism whose feet were beginning to furrow the roads of Provence. The people exercised their sovereignty as they marched. Practices that developed as they marched together produced citizens convinced that assemblies at a primary level should be open to all those of "French nationality," provided, of course, they carried a section card. Spokesmen arose to voice the passions that expressed the "moral needs" of the sovereign people. The cold assembly legislators were invited to manifest due sensitivity. They must be receptive to the emotions of the people. On a spontaneous impulse, there would be declarations of the sacred nature of this "surge of emergent peoples' power." New assembly practices such as these clearly called for a change of scene. In

Marseilles, where people knew how to interpret the force of this deliberative movement, a central committee took on the task of producing a "general
consensus." It would be interesting to know how the Soviets proceeded at
the time of the early Bolsheviks and comrade Lenin. However, the inquiry
pursued by the historians and ethnologists since 1992 has unfortunately not
provided us with any such documentation.

In the aftermath of 1789, in order to set up dialogue between the 1,200
elected members of the Constituent Assembly, who were determined "to
imitate nobody," it was first necessary to establish control over the agenda,
in order to pass new laws and take the necessary financial decisions. How
could one obtain a chance to speak? How could the discussion be focused in
such a way as to keep it egalitarian yet have it proceed by way of a series of
orderly motions? Soon, a number of virtually permanent committees were
created, the operations of which were essential for the new "twenty million"
citizens. Fortunately, many of these mechanisms had already been tried and
tested by the House of Commons of Great Britain, although significant differences remained: for example, the members of the Constituent Assembly
elected themselves a new chairman every two weeks. There was no question
of electing a Speaker for the entire duration of a Parliament, as in England,
where it may remain in place for seven years. In this connection, it would
be useful to set up a comparison relating to different beginnings, particularly the beginnings of London's House of Commons, whose practices involve
a whole parliamentary rhetoric the effects of which, after a succession of
adjustments, still mark the European assemblies in Strasbourg today and are
likely to continue to do so.[6]

How to Compare and Why

In this collaborative comparative approach it is not, nor will it ever be, a
matter of juxtaposing a dash of Japan that in some inexplicable way sums up
the whole of Japan, a flavor of the Circassians to represent the entire mass of
the Caucasus, all in one go, and—just to add a touch of color—two or three
Italian communes, in order to justify writing, in the conclusion to a volume
of the "comparative studies" ilk, "This is how people assembled together in
Italy and invented politics, while in Japan . . . ." That would be to travel far
and wide as dupes, only to resume the society game played by Hellenists,
for whom nothing is more exciting than discovering whether *our* Athenians

---

6 See Guilhaumou 2003, Wahnich 2003, and Brasart 2003.

really experienced "Democracy," real democracy, or (a more refined variant of the same theme) whether it was Solon or Cleisthenes who should be forever honored for having invented politics (*le politique* in French: why a singular noun? Most peculiar . . .).

The eye of a comparatist discerns practices associated with the act of assembling that might very well not have been adopted or that might have engendered other kinds of equality. He or she also discerns practices that may die out: alongside tentative advances and lightning manifestations, some achievements that have won acceptance, possibly over several centuries, seem to have been made possible only thanks to the evanescence of other experiments, now forgotten, never mentioned, gone forever. History, the kind taught in schools and universities, offers us the fascinating study of *our* Greeks, who belong to *us* (or is it the other way around?), without ever considering more modern peoples and aspects of their lives. Anthropology, meanwhile, wakes up comparative every morning, free to flit from culture to culture, gathering its honey wherever the will to assemble has sprouted and bloomed. With its taste for dissonance, anthropology invites us to focus on societies that present contrasts that may seem either excessive or mysterious, depending on the view of the observer who comes upon them. Unchecked by barriers in space or time, anthropology collects them all, separates them out, and goes on to discover others, elsewhere. But why? (For that question resurfaces like an uncheckable weed as soon as scholarship becomes concerned about this discipline and its future). In the first place, because setting a number of experiments in perspective usually reveals areas of intelligibility the value and tonality of which are recognized by both historians of politics[7] and even philosophers, in their own domains of study; second, because a collection of beginnings, observed in the concrete process of their evolution, may make it possible to analyze, as if under a microscope, the components of neighboring configurations, each of which, with its own particular differential features, may help an attentive comparatist to spot the deviation from the norm that distinguishes, among a whole series of possibilities, the particular formula of a microconfiguration of politics.

7   See Rosanvallon 2003.

2

The Gods of Politics in Early Greek Cities*

H ERE, I HAVE DECIDED TO SPEAK of "the gods" rather than "religion." The "gods" know why I have rejected a modern reference to "religion." I confess that I have never held the terms "religious" and "religion" in high esteem. And that is not solely because those terms, with their associations with *religio-religere* and the idea of ritualistic scruples, conjure up certain scruples with regard to cults. No sooner had I won the freedom to embark on research at the Ecole des Hautes Etudes than I began to plot how to escape from the protected territory known as *Sciences religieuses* (Religious Studies).[1] My first collaborative seminar set out to explore the limits of the field of religion. Where did this field begin? And how was it changing before our very eyes? The specialists of that protected territory, a good fifty or so of them, shared a stubborn reluctance to ask fundamental questions about what was conventionally called the religion of the ancient Babylonians, the Old Testament, or the Aztecs. Among the first ten or twelve professorial chairs in Paris, there was even one for Greek religion, the one that I persistently endeavored to shake up in order to develop its full potential, during the period when it served as the basis for my comparative operations. Although the Roman legacy cannot be held entirely to blame, it was through it, its language, and its culture that there was pressure, already in the Christian Augustine, to consider polytheisms as vast *terrae incognitae* that were destined eventually to receive True Religion, whether from Christianity or from Islam. As our experts have established, over three quarters of the world's population are naturally polytheistic. Consider for a moment the eight hundred myriads of deities in Japan, the countless metamorphoses of the deities of Hinduism, the thousands of genies and powers of black Africa. Likewise, the forests and mountain

---

* This chapter is a revision of an article published in *Arion* 12.2 (Fall 2004) 49–66.
1 Cf. Detienne 1968.

ranges of Oceania, the Indian subcontinent, and South America are teeming with pantheons with great clusters of deities.

It is probably fair to say, without fear of contradiction, that on the limitless horizon of polytheisms, monotheism appears as a kind of religious mistake—for these do occur, just as sentimental mistakes do, although the latter fortunately tend to be more short-lived. Polytheistic societies revel in their ignorance of churches and episcopal authorities, whether pastoral or papal. They mock these upstart monotheists for their insistence on "having to believe" and their proselytizing efforts.

As we all know, the field of polytheisms constitutes a vast continent, one that awaits all those wishing to experiment in the world of the possible relations that link divine powers. I will venture into it solely to seek out the gods who speak Greek, who, however, are delighted to be translated and interpreted into other languages. Just as in Japan there are *karni* for ovens, for food, for costumes, and for domestic altars, so too, in Greece the gods are everywhere. So why should they not be there in the political domain?

To uncover the network of these Greek-speaking gods, it was necessary to concentrate less on their individual features and to resist the attraction of their fine appearances, and instead to identify all the different ways in which deities are associated on altars and in sanctuaries. In a polytheistic system, a god is always plural, constituted by the intersection of a variety of attributes. In this sense, a god is conjectural, a figure with many angles and many facets.

Greek culture presents observers with well-established arrangements and organized relations between two or more powers, relations of explicit partnership and complementarity between deities. As Georges Dumézil stressed, any attentive observer cannot fail to note the "structural" aspect of Greek culture. Moreover, it is possible to analyze these networks of relations between the same sets of deities over a full twelve centuries, from Homer right down to Porphyry. This is a wonderful field for experimentation, and I have been exploring it in a work on Apollo.[2] It is a very rich seam, crying out to be exploited.

There may be gods everywhere, but which are the gods of the political domain? What is so particular about them? Is it not rather surprising that there should be any need for gods in a space defined by assembly practices whose major object seems to be the affairs of the human group? What are the gods doing in a space that seems principally concerned with human matters and is devoted to a Common Good (*xunon*) that is the business of all the group members?

---

2 Cf. "Experimenting in the Field of Polytheisms" in this volume.

We can study the beginnings of such phenomena in many different societies. Those that came about in dozens of communities in Italy between the eleventh and the thirteenth centuries owe nothing to those that arose among the Cossacks of Zaporizhia, in quite a different history, or to all those "places for politics" that are detectable in the soil of Magna Graecia or on the shores of the Black Sea. But I believe that the beginnings of the tiny, first Greek cities deserve the full attention of a comparatist-cum-Hellenist, fascinated by the ever-changing colors of their "places for politics," that shimmering quality which the Greeks called *poikilos.*

Let me concentrate on three examples of beginnings in the Greek terrain: the precarious city of the Achaeans who came to besiege the town of Priam, the imaginary city of the Phaeacians; and the early archaeological and material evidence found at Megara Hyblaea, in Sicily, dating from about 730 BCE.

First, the *Iliad.* The Greeks who sailed to Troy hailed from many different places. In the midst of the ships hauled up on to the beach, they created a space where the Achaeans assembled to deliberate together. The spot was known as an *agora*: the word referred at once to the physical place of the assembly, the men who came there to deliberate, and the words that they exchanged there. We also know that this space marked out by the warriors who gathered to speak there contained an *"agora, themis,* and the altars of the gods."[3] Let us, for the moment, leave aside *themis* and all that the word evokes in the way of decisions debated and taken. The most significant point is that altars for the gods were here—for the gods of all the Greeks? Maybe, maybe not. At any rate there are gods in this place, which, by virtue of the series of practices of sharing between the warriors there, may be called a place of "equality."

Next, the Phaeacians. The name of Nausicaa's grandfather was Nausithoos. In the past, he had lived in the neighborhood of the rowdy and violent Cyclopes, who despised the gods and their altars and had no conception of what an assembly, an *agora*, was. They exasperated Nausithoos, who decided to move away and eventually came to found the city of the Phaeacians. He did so as a protofounder of what we, using a Latin word, came to call the "colonies" of Sicily and elsewhere. To be on the safe side, Nausithoos built great ramparts of stone around his city; he shared out parcels of land, for which lots were drawn; and he designed a magnificent *agora*, made of well-hewn stone, flanked by a temple for Poseidon. It was as if this god had an unquestionable right to the rank of *poliad* (or city) deity. Athena, who arrived to guide Odysseus as he made his way to the city of Nausicaa, was careful to

---

3 *Iliad* XI 807. Cf. Detienne 1998a:155.

go no further than a small, sacred grove situated well outside the precinct of Poseidon's realm.[4]

The town laid out on the Phaeacian shore was strangely like the city of Megara Hyblaea, in Sicily, the foundations of which archaeologists have patiently reconstructed. The future city was plotted out on virgin soil by its founder around 730 BCE. In its center, a space was immediately marked out for the *agora*, the public area that would be completed one century later. Another site, close to the *agora*, seems to have been chosen to accommodate several sanctuaries, which were then gradually built. The land of the city founded by Megara was initially divided up into more or less regular allotments, according to the method followed by Nausicaa's grandfather.[5]

Meetings in assembly, for the purpose of deliberation according to the rule of "debating pro and contra," such as those described in the *Iliad*, followed practices with an easily observable ceremonial that makes it possible for us to determine the role and place of the gods within the space of the *agora*. As the great work *Délibération et pouvoir dans les cités grecques* by Françoise Ruzé (1997) describes, from Nestor down to Socrates, the space of deliberative speech took the form of a circle or a semicircle. Whoever wished to speak for "the common good" would advance to the middle, *es meson*, where he would be handed the sceptre that conferred authority upon his words so long as his *agora* (in the sense of speech) concerned what the *Odyssey* calls "a public matter" (*ti dêmion*).[6] It all thus began amid a gathering of warriors, men who set as much store by the art of speech as by the martial arts (which is not the case in all warrior societies). The altar with its gods, set up by the Achaeans at the center of their semicircle of ships, was to be longer lasting than the siege of Troy, for the Greek-speaking gods were to continue to be involved in the founding practices of cities and of these special places devoted to "the political domain." Two divine powers were always directly involved in the planning of a new city. First Apollo, known as a founder, an *Archêgetês*.[7] And hard on his heels came Hestia, the Greek Vesta, with her sacrificial fire. Apollo was the god of Delphi. Any would-be founder had to go to consult him. Apollo was revered as a god of paths and reliable plans, and he liked to accompany human founders, keeping an eye on them. As an architect and a geometrician, Apollo the Founder was the patron of the art of city planning, dividing

---

4 *Odyssey* vi 4–10, Cf. Detienne 1998a:105–106.
5 Cf. Detienne 1998a:108–110.
6 *Odyssey* II 39.
7 Detienne 1998a:84–104, "Prince de la colonization: archégète."

the territory into allotments of land, building roads and sanctuaries (*temenê*), and marking out the space for the *agora*.

There could be no city without an *agora*, no city without altars and sacrificial fire. In many cases, immediately upon disembarking the founder would consecrate an altar to his own Apollo. But an altar was not enough to make a city. There was also a need for sacrificial fire that had been brought from the central altar of the founder's native city.

So Hestia, the deity of fire in general and sacrificial fire in particular, always came along too on the voyage, bringing a seed of fire kept in a cooking pot. Very early on, Hestia, the virgin deity of fire that was never extinguished, was set up to preside over a very public edifice known as the *Prutaneion*, what some might call a town hall, the center of the executive department for Communal Affairs. Hestia represented what you might call "a particular idea of the city." Symbolically she embodied the unity of the multiplicity of individual domestic hearths and altars. She was a figure at once concrete and abstract. With her central altar in the Prytaneum, she presided over the sacrificial commensality that was officially practiced by the magistrates, the *prutaneis* who received their powers as magistrates from her altar, the altar of Hestia.[8] "Political" authority thus came from Hestia; not from Apollo the Founder, nor from any god known as a god "of the city," a poliad god, *polias-polieus*. In this eminently "public" place, Hestia reigned over the complex interplay of what I earlier called "sameness and equality." For this was the place where the multiple configurations of "citizenship" were constructed, all the rights and obligations of those who came forward to speak.

By observing the assembly practices of these early cities, it is not hard to see that they take place in a space in the shape of a circle, or a semi-circle, and that they are peculiar to a space called an *agora*, a fixed space that is common to the greatest possible number of citizens. It is a space that is both common and *public* (*dêmosion* as the Greek puts it). The *agora*, which in Crete is sometimes called the *agora* of the assembled citizens, functions as a deity of effective publicity. Here charges were proclaimed in cases of homicide, and certain benefactions were publicly accepted. These were public applications of speech of a legal nature, and they helped to create something that seems to become essential in the constitution of a "place for politics" in Greece, namely publicity. It was necessary to publicize—make known to all—the decisions taken by a majority of those who set out to deliberate on what we may now call "public affairs" and who aimed to have these decisions observed and

8 Detienne 1998a:107, 113, 116, 163–164, 166–168.

applied by others in their city. To this end, these little cities of between two hundred and five hundred men, with territories of no more than between five and ten square kilometers, at about the same time invented the art of writing on bronze tablets and stone *stêlai*. These were sometimes affixed to walls, sometimes displayed in what were considered to be public places. The intention, sometimes explicitly spelled out in these inscriptions, was to place on view, for all to see, the decrees that had been passed and the decisions that had been taken—"words solidly established" (*thesmoi*), as Solon puts it.[9] For example, in Chios, a narrow island roughly level with Smyrna, an early sixth-century *stêlê* urges the elected magistrates, *in the name of Hestia* to observe the decisions of the people, the *dêmos* of Chios. Inscribing words on *stêlai* and writing on walls were the constitutive practices of "the political domain" in the village-cities that engaged in various forms of assembly. But what with all this talk of public space, publicity, and public opinion, I am perhaps moving too fast, as the gods are now reminding me. Long before the printing press and the wide diffusion of debates in our eighteenth-century Europe of only yesterday, in every village-city there were temples with walls, and sanctuaries with space: and it was there, in the temples of Apollo, Artemis, Hera, Poseidon, and others, that the public documents such as the rules of sacrifice and the decisions of the assembly were *published*, that is to say exhibited, posted up. Temples and sanctuaries were public places, open to all. There was no Holy of Holies; and the so-called priests were annually elected magistrates who were expected to give an account of the spending of public money. The sanctuaries of the *agora*, the temples on the Acropolis, and the altars scattered through the countryside were all public places, places of publicity by decision of the council and the assembly, which could thus make known to all and sundry what they ought to do.

Just as there were gods on the *agora*, on the Acropolis, in the Prytaneum, and in the council chamber, there were gods for becoming a citizen, for all males born from parents who lived in the city territory. Such youths had to be presented to the altars and members of their phratry, and then be accepted into a deme, which was a city in miniature, with its own assemblies, its own sacrifices, its own particular gods, and its own sanctuaries that were used to publicize the decrees passed by the deme members, the *dêmotai*.[10]

---

9 On Hestia and Themis, cf. Detienne 1998a:156–60.

10 For a short introduction to these issues, see Sissa and Detienne 2000:166–207, "Gods at the Heart of Politics."

In a polytheistic society, the gods are everywhere, for sure. But not in a random manner. There are certain domains in which they seem to be concentrated, certain types of experience in which they are organized in unusual or improbable ways. The multiplicity of gods seems to make it possible to think through and form an image of a large number of the activities and problems that men encountered in their social lives. I think we should try to discover whether or not gods, particular gods, were directly involved in what I shall—if I may—call "the autonomy of the political domain in itself."

Let me spell this out. I have described the practices of the deliberative assembly and the repeated and regulated exercises performed by a decision-taking group that progressively comes to think of itself as a unity made from a plurality and that creates for itself this new public space. All these practices sooner or later, depending on the circumstances, played their part in forging the by no means ordinary idea of *the group's sovereignty over itself.* Yes, sovereignty, and I am of course thinking of those first Greek cities, which never needed to behead a sovereign or to abolish an ancien régime. But now, as a careful comparatist, my thoughts also turn to the whole of "traditional" West Africa, which does not appear to have any "public places." Indeed, you could even say that there is no space at all there between the power of the king or royal chieftain and the society, which is organized into clans. The king accumulates in his person all the powers that are disseminated among the clans and lineages. As the Africanist Alfred Adler puts it, in many cases, the sacralized power that is vested in the king leaves no separating gap between his person, which is set about with prohibitions, and the society made up of clans and lineages. This society seems to base its idea of itself on its recognition that the king assumes the (often weighty) privilege of ensuring the society's union with the whole collection of the forces of nature, both visible and invisible. On the one hand, we thus find a society that forms an image of itself through a sacred king; on the other, a society in which a certain idea of the city, Hestia, is formed by a group which, for its part, comes to believe that the sovereignty of this new unit, the city, resides in itself.

It is possible to observe how this "sovereignty of the group over itself" operates in practice. And the gods are directly involved. Let us consider a concrete case. At the end of the sixth century, somewhere in the mountains of Crete, a little city engaged a scribe, for a large fee. His name was Spensithius, and he was an expert in purple letters, that is to say Phoenician writing. His contract specified that he should set down in writing all public matters (*dêmosia*), or, to be more precise, both the affairs of the gods and the affairs of men. The two were kept clearly separate, as it attested by scores of epigraphical documents. The contract also stated that Spensithius of Crete should be responsible for the management of public sacrifices, those known as "common" or "ancestral," which were an essential part of the communal affairs of any city.[11] As all Hellenists know, the ritual calendar, with all its information, relayed about 50 percent of the so-called laws of Solon. But the essential point for me is that "the affairs of the gods," the first section of "public matters," were debated, discussed, and decided in the assembly and—moreover—in the first part of the assembly. The assembly decided by a majority vote how the new calendar should be organized and the order in which the various gods would be honored. So the sovereignty of the group over itself clearly also covered its gods and their affairs. I should perhaps interject, in passing, that there was a hierarchy in the way that things were ordered: the affairs of the gods were dealt with first, and by this select circle of citizens from long-established families. But why and how did mortals, human beings, gain such a hold over "the affairs of the gods"? It turns out that among these people, "our" Greeks, the gods, the gods of Olympus and the whole world, never thought of inventing such a thing as a "city." Cities were an invention of men, of mortals, and one fine day the gods woke up to this fact. In no time, they were jostling at the gate, clamoring for the privileges of a so-called poliad deity—as it were, a better paid "chair" than an ordinary seat in the pantheon.

Of all the human activities, politics was thus the one that was specifically constructed by human beings: politics, the government of humans by humans, a government with full sovereignty and, what is more, which sought to affirm that autonomy, in other words was "a law unto itself."

The autonomy of the political domain did not simply fall from the sky. It was problematic, fragile, had to be invented by whatever available means. To come back to this field in which so much still remains to be done, I would like, finally, to suggest that a number of important aspects of action, decision, and the strategies of politics took shape and were analyzed with reference to the divine powers. Hestia, who represented such a complex category, is certainly one of them. I also believe that the Aphrodite-Ares pair, which is of major importance and represents the relationship between the rituals of warfare on the one hand and harmony and concord on the other, introduces a set of major tensions that must be taken into account in any analysis of the political field.

---

11 See van Effenterre and Ruzé 1994.

The so-called Aphrodite of Magistrates is no zoological curiosity, but is, on the contrary, central to thought about the nature of the council and the concept of decision and power to deliberate upon communal matters. The all-too-Greek aspects of those concepts, which may well try your patience, lead us to a whole micropantheon which spoke solely of the political domain.

Now, at the end of this conversation (or *conversari*), allow me to return to the subject of comparison and the question of what it is possible to compare. It would be mistaken to take either the combination of politics and religion or that of theology and politics or even that of politics and ritual as some kind of universal standard. "Politics" and "Religion" are no more than dry encyclopedia entries. The modernity of the Shinto of the Meiji was invented using the deification and cult of a top-hatted emperor who opened electric power stations and new railway networks. The "minister of divine affairs" collaborated with the department of "National Studies" to redefine the relations between Buddhists, Confucians, and Shintoists of a variety of persuasions. This was in the early twentieth century. It was an extraordinary politicoreligious configuration, impossible to view in perspective until such time as an attempt was made to analyze its components and the formation of its successive strata. Shinto was reason enough, at the time. No doubt, but what kind of reason? And on the basis of what practices was it constructed? And what about the Christian West? Does it justify liberated minds declaring that politics were invented in the religious domain, and—besides—which religious domain? Similarly, even if, as a hasty and preliminary hypothesis, in ancient Rome religious power legitimated political power, is it not advisable to work with historians who can analyze the extremely complex system of assemblies and the interaction of what the Romans called *auctoritas* and *inauguratio*? Rome may have introduced citizen gods and various kinds of contracts between men and the gods, but how and in the course of what parallel or successive experiences did the domain of politics take shape there?

What I wish to suggest is that this kind of experimental and constructive comparison, practiced by historians in collaboration with anthropologists, may provide a useful way to probe the complexity of societies, such as present-day Israel (which is but one of many), which draw attention to the extreme fragility of what we call the "political domain." It was much the same in the past. Nothing much has changed.

WORKS CITED

Abélès, M. 1983. *Le lieu du politique*. Paris.

———. 2003. "Revenir chez les Ochollo." In Detienne 2003b:393–413.

Ackerman, R. 1987. *J. G. Frazer: His Life and Work*. Cambridge.

Allen, T. W., Halliday, W. R., and Sikes, E. E. 1936. *The Homeric Hymns*. 2nd ed. Oxford.

Altherr-Charon, A., and Bérard, C. 1980. "Erétrie, l'organisation de l'espace et la formation d'une cité grecque." *L'Archéologie d'aujourd'hui* (ed. A. Schnapp) 229–249. Paris.

Angiolillo, S. 1981. "La visita di Dioniso a Ikarios nelle ceramica attica: Appunti sulla politica culturale pisistratea." *Dialoghi di archeologia* 1:13–22

Attias, J.-C., and Benbassa, E. 2001. *Israël: La terre et le sacré*. 2nd ed. revised. Paris.

Balestrazzi, E. d. F. 1980–81. "L'Agyieus e la città." *Atti del Centro ricerche e documentazione sull'antichità classica* 11: 93–108.

Barrès, M. 1899. "La Terre et les Morts (sur quelles réalités fonder la conscience française)." *Ligue de la Patrie Française, Troisième Conférence, March 10, 1899*. Paris.

Becker, C. 1937. *Das Bild des Weges und verwandte Vorstellungen im frühgriechischen Denker*. Hermes Einzelschriften 4. Berlin.

Belfiore, E. 1986. "Wine and Catharsis of the Emotions in Plato's Laws." *Classical Quarterly* 36:421–437.

Bérard, C. 1971. "Architecture érétrienne et mythologie delphique." *Antike Kunst* 14:59–73.

Bernardini, Paola Angeli, ed. 2000. *Presenza e funzione della città di Tebe nella cultura greca*. Pisa.

Biers, W. R., and Boyd, T. D. 1982. "Ikarion in Attica: 1888–1981." *Hesperia* 51:1–18.

Bodéüs. R. 1992. *Aristote et la théologie des vivants immortels*. Paris.

Bolton, J. D. P. 1962. *Aristeas of Proconnesus*. Oxford.

Borgeaud, P. 2004. *Aux origines de l'histoire des religions*. Paris.

Boyancé, P. 1972. *Le Culte des Muses chez les philosophes grecs*. 2nd ed. Paris.

Brasart, P. 2003. "Des commons au Manège: Effets d'écho en Chambre sourde." In Detienne 2003b:373–389.

Braudel, F. 1986. *L'identité de la France*. 3 vols. Paris.

Bravo, B. 1988. "Dieu et les dieux chez F. Creuzer et F. G. Welcker: L'impensable polythéisme." *L'Impensable Polythéisme* (ed. F. Schmidt) 375–424. Paris.

Breglia Pulci Doria, L. 1986. "Demeter Erinys Tilphusa tra Poseidon e Ares." *Les grandes figures religieuses. Fonctionnement pratique et symbolique dans l'Antiquité, Besançon 25-26 avril 1984.* 107–126. Paris.

Brulé, P. 1987. *La Fille d'Athènes: La Religion des filles à Athènes à l'époque classique*. Paris.

Bruneau, P. 1970. *Recherches sur les cultes de Délos à l'époque hellénistique et à l'époque classique*. Paris.

———. 1976. "Communication." *Revue des études grecques* 89:xiii ff.

Boffo, L. 1978. "La lettera di Dario I a Gadata: I privilegi del tempio di Apollo a Magnesia sul Meandro." *Bullettino dell'Istituto di diritto romano 'Vittorio Scialoja'* 20:267–303.

Burkert, W. 1985. *Greek Religion*. Trans. J. Raffan. Cambridge, MA.

Calame, C. 1990. *Thésée et l'imaginaire athénien*. Lausanne.

Cartry, M., and Detienne, M., eds. 1996. *Destins de meurtriers*. Paris.

Casevitz, M. 1985. *Le vocabulaire de la colonisation en grec ancien*. Paris.

Chantraine, P. 1968-80. *Dictionnaire étymologique de la langue grecque*. 4 vols. Paris

Charachidzè, G. 1968. *Le système religieux de la Géorgie païenne: Analyse structurelle d'une civilisation*. Paris.

Clay, J. S. 1989. *The Politics of Olympus: Form and Meaning in the Major Homeric Hymns.* Princeton.

Copans, J. 1996. *Introduction à l'ethnologie et à l'anthropologie.* Paris.

Curtius, E. 1894. "Zur Geschichte des Wegebaus bei den Griechen." *Gesammelte Abhandlungen.* 1:1–116. Berlin.

de la Boullaye, H. P. 1922. *L'étude comparée des religions.* Vol. 1. Paris.

de Romilly, J., and Vernant, J.-P. 2000. *Pour l'amour du grec.* Paris.

Defradas, J. 1972. *Les thèmes de la propagande delphique.* 2nd ed. Paris.

Delcourt, M. 1955. *L'Oracle de Delphes.* Paris.

Delumeau, J.-P. 2003. "De l'assemblé précommunale au temps des conseils. En Italie centrale." In Detienne 2003b:213–228

Detienne, M. 1968a. "La phalange. Problèmes et controverses." *Problèmes de la guerre en Grèce ancienne* (ed. J.-P. Vernant) 119–142. Paris

———. 1968b. "Recherches comparatives sur le problème du char." With P. Garelli, E. Cassin, and J. Gernet. *Problèmes de la guerre en Grèce ancienne* (ed. J.-P. Vernant) 289–318. Paris

———. 1975. "Les Grecs ne sont pas comme les autres." *Critique* 332:3–24.

———. 1978. "La mythologie scandaleuse." *Traverses* 12:3–19.

———. 1984. "Au commencement était le corps des dieux." Preface to *Les dieux de la Grèce: La figure du divin au miroir de l'esprit grec* (W. F. Otto) 7–19. Paris.

———. 1985a. "La Cité en son autonomie. Autour d'Hestia." *Quaderni di Storia* 22:59–78.

———. 1985b. "Un Polythéism Récrit. Entre Dionysos et Apollon: Mort et vie d'Orphée." *Archives des sciences sociales des religions* 59:65–75.

———. 1986. "Apollo und Dionysos in der griechischen Religion." *Die Restauration der Götter. Antike Religion und Neo-Paganismus* (ed. R. Faber and R. Schlesier) 124–132. Würzburg.

———. 1989a. *Dionysos at Large.* Trans. A. Goldhammer. Cambridge, MA.

———. 1989b. *L'Écriture d'Orphée.* Paris.

———, ed. 1990. *Tracés de fondation.* Paris-Louvain.

———. 1994a. *The Gardens of Adonis.* Trans. Janet Lloyd. 2nd ed. Princeton.

———, ed. 1994b. *Transcrire les mythologies: Tradition, écriture. historicité.* Paris.

———. 1996. *The Masters of Truth in Archaic Greece.* Trans. Janet Lloyd. New York.

———. 1998a. *Apollon le couteau à la main: Une approche expérimentale du polythéisme grec.* Paris.

———. 1998b. *Dionysos mis à mort.* Paris.

———. 2000a. "Avec ou sans écriture." Introd. to "Les Ecritures." *Science de l'Homme et de la Société.* Department letter, no. 60.

———. 2000b. *Comparer l'incomparable.* Paris.

———. 2001. "Back to the Village: A Tropism of Hellenists?" *History of Religions* 41:99–113.

———. 2002a. "L'art de construire des comparables: Entre historiens et anthropologues." *Critique internationale* 14:68–78.

———. 2002c. "Murderous Identity: Anthropology, History, and the Art of Constructing Comparables." *Common Knowledge* 8:178–187.

———. 2003a. *Comment être autochtone: Du pur athénien au Français raciné.* Paris.

———, ed., 2003b. *Qui veut prendre la parole?* Paris.

———. 2003c. *The Writing of Orpheus: Greek Myth in Cultural Context.* Trans. Janet Lloyd. Baltimore.

———. 2005. *Les Grecs et nous: Une anthropologie comparée de la Grèce ancienne.* Paris.

Detienne, M., and J.-P. Vernant. 1978. *Cunning Intelligence in Greek Culture and Society.* Trans. Janet Lloyd. Sussex.

Devyver, André. 1973. *Le sang épuré: Les préjugés de race chez les gentilshommes français de l'Ancien Régime, 1550-1720.* Brussels.

Dixsaut, M., ed. 1995. *Querelle autour de 'La Naissance de la tragédie.'* Trans. M. Cohen-Halami, H. Poitevin, and M. Marcuzzi. Paris.

Duchet, M. 1985. *Le partage des savoirs.* Paris.

Dumézil, G. 1949. *L'héritage indo-européen à Rome.* Paris.

———. 1952. *Les dieux des Indo-Européens.* Paris.

———. 1954. *Rituels indo-européens à Rome.* Paris.

———. 1966. *La religion romaine archaïque*. Paris.

———. 1967. "A propos des aspects de la fonction guerrière." *Cahiers pour l'Analyse, Cercle d'epistémologie de l' E. N. S. 7*. Paris.

———. 1968. *Problèmes et méthodes d'Histoire des Religions*. Paris.

———. 1973. *Mythe et Epopée*. Vol. 3, *Histoires romaines*. Paris.

———. 1977. *Les dieux souverains des Indo-Européens*. Paris.

Dumont, L. 1957. *Une sous-caste de l'Inde du Sud: Organisation sociale et religion des Pramalai Kallar*. Paris.

Durand, J.-L. 1986. *Sacrifice et labour en Grèce ancienne*. Paris.

Durkheim, E. 1937. *Les règles de la méthode sociologique*. Repr., 11th ed. 2002. Paris.

Durkheim, E. 1975. *Textes*. Ed. V. Karády. Vol. 3. Paris.

Eribon, D., and Lévi-Strauss, C. 1984. *De près et de loin*. Paris.

Frontisi-Ducroux, F. 1986. *La cithare d'Achille*. Rome.

Furet, F. 1982. *L'Atelier de l'histoire*. Paris.

Geertz, C. 1983. *Local Knowledge: Further Essays in Interpretative Anthropology*. New York.

Georgoudi, S. 1986. "Pratiques sacrificielles grecques. Divinités et victimes animales." *Annuaire de l'École pratique des Hautes Études, Sciences religieuses* 95:286–292.

———. 2001. "Ancêtres de Sélinonte et d'ailleurs: Le cas des tritopatores." *Les Pierres de l'offrande: Autour de l'oeuvre de Christoph W. Clairmont* 152–163. Zurich.

Gernet, L. 1932. "You-you. En marge d'Hérodote." *Cinquantenaire de la Faculté des Lettres d'Alger.* 1–12. Algiers.

Glaser, H. 1978. *The Cultural Roots of National Socialism*. Trans. E. A. Menze. Austin.

Goldschmidt, V. 1970. *Questions platoniciennes*. Paris.

Graf, F. 1974. "Das Kollegium der Molpoi von Olbia." *Museum Helveticum* 31:209–215.

———. 1979. "Apollon Delphinios." *Museum Helveticum* 36:2–22.

Grégoire, H., Goossens, R., and Mathieu, M. 1949. *Asklépios, Apollon Smintheus et Rudra*. Brussels.

Gründer, K., ed. 1969. *Der Streit um Nietzsches 'Geburt der Tragödie' von E. Rohde, R. Wagner, U. von Wilamowitz-Möllendorff*. Hildesheim.

Guilhaumou, J. 2003. "Un argument saisi dans le mouvement démocratique, la souveraineté délibérante, à Marseille." In Detienne 2003b:329–348.

Haar, M. 1993. *Nietzsche et la métaphysique*. Paris.

Hellmann, M.-C. 1988. "A propos d'un lexique de termes d'architecture grecque." *Comptes et inventaires dans la cité grecque* (ed. D. Knoepfler) 239–261. Neuchâtel-Geneva.

Humbert, J. 1959. *Homère: Hymnes*. Paris.

Izard, M., and Bonte. P., eds. 1991. *Dictionnaire de l'ethnologie et de l'anthropologie*. Paris.

Jacob, C. 1993. "Paysage et bois sacré: Alsos dans la Périégèse de la Grèce de Pausanias." *Les Bois sacrés* (ed. O. de Cazenove and J. Scheid) 31–44. Coll. du Centre J. Bérard 10. Naples.

Jameson, M. H., Jordan, D. R., and Kotansky, R. D. 1993. *A 'lex sacra' from Selinous*. Durham.

Janko, R. 1986. "The Shield of Heracles and the Legend of Cycnus." *Classical Quarterly* 36:38–59.

Jeanmaire, H. 1978. *Dionysos: Histoire du culte de Bacchus: l'orgiasme dans l'antiquité et les temps modernes, origine du théâtre en Grèce, orphisme et mystique dionysiaque, évolution du dionysisme après Alexandre*. Paris.

Jouan, F., and Van Looy, H., eds. 2000. *Euripide*. Vol. 8.2, *Fragments*. Paris.

Jouanna, J. 1996. "Le Vin et la médecine dans la Grèce ancienne." *Revue des études grecques* 109:410–34

Judeich, W. 1898. "Inschriften." *Altertümer von Hierapolis* (ed. C. Humann, et al.) 67–180. Jahrbuch des Kaiserlich Deutschen Archäologischen Instituts. Ergänzungsheft 4. Berlin.

Kern, O. 1900. *Die Inschriften von Magnesia am Maeander*. Berlin.

Krappe, A. H. 1942. "ΑΠΟΛΛΩΝ ΚΥΚΝΟΣ." *Classical Philology* 37:353–370.

Kraus, T. 1960. *Hekate*. Heidelberg.

Lebedynsky, I. 2003. "Les Cosaques, rites et metamorphoses d'une démocratie guerrière." In Detienne 2003b:147–170.

Lenclud, G. 1987. "Anthropologie et histoire, hier et aujourd'hui en France." *Ethnologies en miroir: La France et les pays de langue allemande* (ed. I. Chiva and U. Jeggle) 35–66. Paris.

Létoublon, F. 1985. *Il allait, pareil à la nuit: Les verbes de mouvement en grec; supplétisme et aspect verbal.* Paris.

Lévi-Strauss, C. 1968. "Religions comparées des peuples sans écriture." *Problèmes et méthodes d'histoire des religions.* 1–7. Paris.

———. 1995. *The Story of Lynx.* Trans. Catherine Tihanyi. Chicago.

Liberski-Bagnoud, D. 2002. *Les dieux du territoire: Penser autrement la généalogie.* Paris.

Linke, U. 1999. *Blood and Nation: The European Aesthetics of Race.* Philadelphia.

Loraux, N. 1981. *L'Invention d'Athènes: Histoire de l'oraison funèbre dans la 'cité classique.'* Paris.

Losonczy, A. M., and Zempleni, A. 1991. "Anthropologie de la 'patrie': Le patriotisme hongrois." *Terrain* 17:29–38.

Malkin, I. 1987. *Religion and Colonization in Ancient Greece.* Leiden.

Masson, O. 1967. "Une inscription thessalienne archaïque relative à la construction d'un edifice." *Bulletin de correspondance hellénique* 92:97–102.

Meiggs, R., and Lewis, D. 1975. *A Selection of Greek Historical Inscriptions to the end of the 5th Century BC.* Oxford.

Meyer, E. 1963. "Pythion." *Paulys Realencyclopädie der classischen Altertumswissenschaft.* Stuttgart.

Meyerson, I., ed. 1973. *Problèmes de la personne.* Paris.

Miller, A. M. 1986. *From Delos to Delphi: A Literary Study of the Homeric Hymns to Apollo.* Leiden.

Morelli, D. 1959. *I culti in Rodi.* Pisa.

Morgan, L. H. 1877. *Ancient Society.* Repr. Tucson, 1985. New York and Chicago.

Nora, P. 1997. "L'Histoire de France de Lavisse." *Les Lieux de Mémoire* (ed. P. Nora) 1:851–891. Paris.

Pépin, J. 1971. *Idées grecques sur l'homme et sur dieu.* Paris.

Petre, Z. 1979. "Trophonios ou l'Architecte: A propos du statut des techniciens dans la cité grecque." *Studii Classiche* 18:23–37.

Pouilloux, J. 1983. "La voie officielle d'accès au stade à Delphes." *Bulletin de correspondance hellénique* 107:217–219.

Redon, O. 2003. "Parole, témoignage, décision dans les assemblées communales en Toscane méridionale aux XIIe–XIIIe siècles." In Detienne 2003b:243–255.

Ritti, T. 1985. *Fonti letterarie ed epigrafiche: Hierapolis Scavi e ricerche.* Vol. 1. Rome.

Robert, F. 1976. "Artémis et Athéna." *Recueil Plassart: études sur l'antiquité grecque offertes à André Plassart par ses collègues de la Sorbonne.* 135–157. Paris.

Robert, J., and Robert, L. 1981. "Bulletin épigraphique." *Revue des études grecques* 94:467, no. 597.

Robert, L. 1950. "Inscriptions de l'Hellespont et de la Propontide." *Hellenica* 9:78–97.

———. 1977. "Documents d'Asie Mineure." *Bulletin de correspondance Hellénique* 101:43–132.

———. 1978. "Documents d'Asie Mineure, V–XVII." *Bulletin de correspondance Hellénique* 102:395–543.

Robichez, J. 1997. *Les Origines de la France.* XIIe Colloque du Conseil scientifique du Front National. Saint Cloud, France.

Robinson, D. M. 1948. "Three New Inscriptions from the Deme of Ikaria." *Hesperia* 17:141–43.

Roesch, P. 1977. "Onchestos, capitale de l'État fédéral Béotien." *Cahiers d'Histoire* 22:82–83.

Rohde, E. 1925. *Psyche.* Trans. W. B. Hillis. New York.

Romano, I. B. 1982. "The Archaic Statue of Dionysos from Ikarion." *Hesperia* 51:398–409

Rosanvallon, P. 2003. "Les vertus d'un comparatisme dérangeant." In Detienne 2003b:7–11.

Rosetti, G. 2003. "Entre Pise et Milan." In Detienne 2003b:229–241.

Roussel, P. 1934. "Un nouveau document concernant le *génos* des ΚΗΡΥΚΕΣ." *Annuaire de l'Institut d'Histoire orientale et slave.* Brussels. 819–834.

Roux, G. 1964. "Sur deux passages de l'hymne homérique à Apollon." *Revue des études grecques* 77:7–22.

———. 1966. "Testimonia Delphica I: Notes sur l'Hymne homérique à Apollon, vers 298." *Revue des Études grecques* 79:1–5.

———. 1976. *Delphes: Son oracle et ses dieux*. Paris.

———. 1979. *L'amphictionie de Delphes et le temple d'Apollon au IVe siècle*. Lyon and Paris.

Ruzé, F. 1997. *Délibération et pouvoir dans les cités grecques*. Paris.

———. 2000. "Les premières manifestations de la citoyenneté en Grèce." *Invention et réinvention de la citoyenneté* (ed. C. Fiévet) 19–28. Aubertin, France.

Salviat, F., and Servais, J. 1964. "Stèle indicatrice thasienne trouvée au sanctuaire d'Aliki." *Bulletin de correspondance hellénique* 88:267–287.

Schachter, A. 1986. *Cults of Boiotia 2: Herakles to Poseidon*. Bulletin of the Institute of Classical Studies, Suppl. 38,2. London.

Schamp, J. 1981. "Apollon prophète par la pierre." *Revue belge de philologie et d'histoire* 59:29–49.

Scheid, J. 1983. "Georges Dumézil et la méthode expérimentale." *Opus* 2:343–354.

Schneider, P. 1987. "Zur topographie der heiligen Strasse von Milet nach Didyma." *Archäologische Anzeiger* (1987):101–129

Servais, J. 1967. "ΣΤΕΜΜΑΤ' ΕΧΩΝ ΕΝ ΧΕΡΣΙΝ." *L'Antiquité Classique* 36:415–456.

Simondon, M. 1982. *La mémoire et l'oubli dans la pensée grecque jusqu'à la fin du Ve siècle avant J. C*. Paris.

Sissa, G., and Detienne, M. 2000. *The Daily Life of the Greek Gods*. Trans. Janet Lloyd. Stanford.

Snell, B. 1938. "Identifikationen von Pindarbruchstücken." *Hermes* 73:424–439.

Sokolowski, F. 1955. *Lois sacrées d'Asie Mineure*. Paris.

———. 1962. *Lois sacrées des cités grecques*. Supplément. Paris.

———. 1969. *Lois sacrées des cités grecques*. Paris.

Solders, S. 1935. "Der ursprungliche Apollo." *Archiv für Religionswissenschaft* 32:142–155.

Sourvinou-lnwood, C. 1979. "The Myth of the First Temples at Delphi." *Classical Quarterly* 29:231–251.

Taylor, C. 1992. *Multiculturalism and "*The Politics of Recognition*"*. Princeton.

Tréheux, J. 1953. "La réalité historique des offrandes hyperboréennes." *Studies Presented to D. M. Robinson*. 2:758–774. St. Louis, Missouri.

Valensi, L. 2002. "L'exercice de la comparaison au plus proche, à distance: Le cas des sociétés plurielles." *Annales, histoire, sciences sociales* 57:27–30.

van Effenterre, H., and Ruzé, F. 1994. *Nomima: recueil d'inscriptions politiques et juridiques de l'archaïsme grec*. Vol. 1. Rome.

Vernant, J.-P. 1983. *Myth and Thought among the Greeks*. London.

Vian, F. 1945. "Le combat d'Héraklès et de Kyknos." *Revue des études anciennes* 47:5–32.

———. 1963. *Les origines de Thébes: Cadmos et les Spartes*. Paris.

Wahnich, S. 2003. "Recevoir et traduire la voix du peuple." In Detienne 2003b:349–372.

Index